PSYCHOPANNYCHIA

The Sleep of the Soul

John Calvin

Ichthus Publications · Apollo, Pennsylvania

The text for this reprint edition is extracted from the 1851 edition of the *Tracts and Treatises in Defense of the Reformed Faith*, Volume III, published by the Calvin Translation Society in Edinburgh. Spelling, language, grammar, and punctuation have been gently updated for the modern reader.

Originally written in 1534 and published as *Psychopannychia. Or, A Refutation of the Error Entertained by Some Unskilful Persons, Who Ignorantly Imagine that in the Interval Between Death and the Judgment the Soul Sleeps. Together with an Explanation of the Condition and Life of the Soul After this Present Life.*

All rights reserved. No part of this publication may be reproduced, stored in a retrieval system, or transmitted, in any form or by any means, electronic, mechanical, photocopying, recording or otherwise, without prior permission of the publisher or the Copyright Licensing Agency.

Our goal is to provide high-quality, thought-provoking books that foster encouragement and spiritual growth. For more information regarding bulk purchases, other IP books, or our publishing services, visit us online or write to support@ichthuspublications.com.

Cover image licensed by Shutterstock.com.

Printed in the United States of America

ISBN: 978-1-946971-45-6

www.ichthuspublications.com

Contents

Translator's Note
// v //

Preface by John Calvin to a Friend
// ix //

To the Reader
// xiii //

Psychopannychia: The Sleep of the Soul
// 19 //

Translator's Note

The title of *Psychopannychia* derived from Greek words which signify "the sleep of the soul;" the object of the tract being to show, partly from reason, but more especially from Scripture, that there is no such sleep. It was originally published in 1534, when Calvin was twenty-five years of age, and is, consequently, with the exception of the Commentary on the *De Clementia* of Seneca, published in 1532, the earliest of all his writings, and two years earlier than the *Institutes*, the first known edition of which appeared in 1536. It thus possesses, especially to those who delight to trace the progress of a master mind, an interest additional to that which its merit gives it.

The figment which it refutes is said by Calvin to be of Arabian origin, but was first brought prominently into notice by some of the wildest fanatics among the Anabaptists, for whom everything new and monstrous appears to have had an irresistible attraction. In more modern times, attempts have been made to give it a philosophical shape, as a necessary corollary from the dogma of Materialism advocated by Priestley and others.

It would seem that the figment, wild and irrational though it is, had made considerable progress at an early period of the Reformation, and counted numerous converts, not merely among the fanatics who had revived it, but in more respectable quarters, where better things might have been expected.

One is puzzled to understand why it should have been received with so much favor; for the idea which it suggests, so far from being attractive, is naturally revolting. It was probably welcomed, not so much for its own sake, as for the great assistance which it was supposed capable of giving in the Roman Catholic controversy. Were it once established that the soul falls asleep at death, and will not awake to consciousness till again united to the body at the resurrection, the pope would forthwith be excluded from the larger half of his domain, and deprived of the most lucrative branches of his trade! There would neither be saints to whom divine honors could be paid, nor purgatory out of which poor souls might be delivered with more or less expedition, according to the number of well-paid masses that were said for them!

If the cordial reception given to the dogma was owing to the collateral benefit thus supposed to be derived from it, it only adds another to the many instances in which blind man would arrogantly give lessons to his Maker, and arrange the world on a better plan than His infinite wisdom has devised. Because it would furnish a triumphant refutation of Popish legends and fictions—the soul must be made to perish with the body, and a common ruin overtake both!

It would appear that the subject had attracted attention in England, for we find that the tract was translated in the reign of Queen Elizabeth. The title-page is as follows:

> A Treatise of the Immortality of the Soul, by which it is proved that souls after the departure of the bodies are awake and do live: against those that think they do sleep. By JOHN CALVIN. Translated out of French by Tho. Stocker.

It was "Imprinted by John Day. London, 1581."

In the *Psychopannychia*, Calvin, knowing the kind of people he had to deal with, accommodates himself to their capacities; and instead of entering largely into speculative disquisitions which the subject seems to suggest, and to which the metaphysical cast of his own mind must have strongly inclined him, dwells primarily on the *scriptural argument*—carefully examining all the passages which the advocates of the dogma had adduced as favorable to their view, and adducing others by which it is completely overthrown. If by the adoption of this plan, the tract loses somewhat in point of philosophical exactness, it gains much in richness of scriptural illustration; and proves that, even at this early period, in writing his first theological publication, Calvin gave promise of the almost unrivaled excellence to which he ultimately trained as a commentator.

Henry Beveridge
May 1851

Preface by John Calvin to a Friend

Long ago, when certain pious persons invited, and even urged me, to publish something for the purpose of repressing the extravagance of those who, alike ignorantly and tumultuously, maintain that the soul dies or sleeps, I could not be induced by all their urgency, so averse did I feel to engage in that kind of dispute. At that time, indeed, I was not without excuse, partly because I hoped that that absurd dogma would soon vanish of its own accord, or at least be confined to a few triflers; partly because I did not think it expedient to engage with a party whose camp and weapons and stratagems I was scarcely acquainted with. For, as yet, nothing had reached me except murmurs and hoarse sounds, so that, to engage with those who had not yet come forth into the arena, seemed to be nothing better than blindly striking the air. The result, however, has been different from what I hoped. These babblers have so actively exerted themselves, that they have already drawn thousands into their insanity.

And even the error itself has, I see, been aggravated. At first, some only vaguely alleged that the soul sleeps, without defining what they wished to be understood by "sleep." Afterwards arose those ψυχοκονοι (*psuchokonoi*), who murder Souls, though without inflicting a wound. The error of the former, indeed, was not to be borne; but I think that the madness of the latter ought to be severely repressed. Both are unsupported by reason and judgment; but it is not so easy to persuade others of this without openly refuting their vanity, and exposing it, so to speak, to their face. This is only to be done by exhibiting it as it appears in their writings. They are said to circulate their follies in a kind of tracts, which I have never happened to see. I have only received some notes from a friend, who had taken down what he had cursorily heard from their lips, or collected by some other means.

Although one reason for my not writing has been partially removed by these notes, the other still remains. However, while the men by whispers, and a garrulity for which they are remarkable, stealthily insinuate themselves, and ensnare no fewer in their error than the circulation of printed books could enable them to do, I feel that I could not well defend myself from the charge of being a traitor to the Truth were I, in such urgent circumstances, to keep back and remain silent! And, while I trust that my labor will be of the greatest use to the more unskillful and less experienced, and not without some use also to the moderately instructed who have given some slight attention to the subject, I will not hesitate to give a reason of my faith to all the good—not such a reason, perhaps, as may fully equip them both for defense and for carrying the war into the enemies' camp, but such a one as will not leave them altogether unarmed. Had the importunity of these men in circulating their dreams among the vulgar allowed me, I would willingly have declined a contest of this nature, in which the fruit gained is not equal to the labor expended, this being one of the cases to which the Apostle's exhortation to be soberly wise particularly applies. But though we long for this soberness, they will not allow us to employ it. Still, my endeavor will be to treat the subject with moderation, and keep it within due bounds.

I wish some other method of cutting away the evil, which makes far too much progress, had been devised, so as to prevent it from gaining ground daily, and eating in like a cancer. Nor does it now appear for the first time; for we read that it originated with some Arabs, who maintained that "The soul dies with the body, and that both rise again at the Day of Judgment" (Euseb. *Eccl. Hist.* lib. 6 c. 36; Aug. *lib. de Haeres.* c. 83, dist. 16; John 2). Some time after, John, Bishop of Rome, broached it, and was forced to recant by the Theological Faculty of Paris (Gerson in *Sermone Pasch. priore*). It lay smoldering for some ages, but has lately begun to send forth sparks, being stirred up by some dregs of Anabaptists. These, spread abroad far and wide, have kindled torches—and would that they were soon extinguished by that voluntary rain which the Lord hath set apart for his inheritance!

I will plead the cause without hatred to any person, without personal affront to any man, in short, without any bitterness of invective, so that no one shall be able to complain of being hurt, or even slightly offended. And yet, in the present day, persons may be seen giving full scope to a carping, biting, scoffing temper, who, if you were only to lay a finger on them, would make a lamentable outcry that "the unity of the Church is rent in pieces, and charity violated!" To such let this be our answer: *First*, that we acknowledge no unity except in Christ; no charity of which He is not the bond; and that, therefore, the chief point in preserving charity is to maintain faith sacred and entire. *Secondly*, that this discussion may proceed without any violation of charity, provided the ears with which they listen correspond with the tongue which I employ.

To you, Honored Sir, I have, thought it right to dedicate this small tract on many accounts, but on one account especially: because I see that, amid those tumults of vain opinions with which giddy spirits disturb the peace of the Church, you stand firm and complete in prudence and moderation.

Orleans, 1534

To the Reader

On again reading this discussion, I observe that, in the heat of argument, some rather severe and harsh expressions have escaped me, which may, perhaps, give offense to delicate ears; and as I know that there are some good men into whose minds some part of this dogma has been instilled, either from excessive credulity or ignorance of Scripture, with which at the time they were not armed so as to be able to resist, I am unwilling to give them offense so far as they will allow me, since they are neither perverse nor malicious in their error. I wish, therefore, to warn such beforehand not to take anything said as an affront to themselves, but to understand that, whenever I use some freedom of speech, I am referring to the nefarious herd of Anabaptists, from whose fountain this noxious stream did, as I observed, first flow, and against whom nothing I have said equals their deserts. If I am to have a future fight with them, I am determined they shall find me, if not a very skillful, yet certainly a firm, and as I dare promise, by God's grace, an invincible defender of the Truth. And yet against them I have not given immoderate vent to my bile, having constantly refrained from all pertness and petulance of speech; tempering my pen so as to be fitter for teaching than forcing, and yet able to draw such as are unwilling to be led. It was certainly much more my intention to bring all back into the right way, than to provoke them to anger.

All who are to read, I exhort and beseech by the Name of God, and of our Lord Jesus Christ, that they bring an impartial judgment and a mind prepared as it were to be the seat of truth. I am aware of the power which novelty has to tickle the ears of certain persons: but we ought to reflect that "Truth has only one voice"—that which proceeds from the lips of our Lord. To Him alone ought we to open our ears when the doctrine of salvation is in question, while to all others we should keep them shut. His word, I say, is not new, but that which was from the beginning, is, and always shall be. And as those err who, when the word of God, which had been laid aside through perverse custom or sloth, is brought to light, charge it with novelty; so they err, in the other direction, who are like reeds driven by the wind, nay, nod and bend at the slightest breeze! When we speak of learning Christ, do we mean that we are to lend an ear, without regard to the word of God, to any doctrine even though true? If you receive it as from man, will you not embrace falsehood with the same facility? For what has man of his own save vanity?

Such was not the conduct of those who, when they had received the word, searched the Scriptures to see whether these things were so (Acts 17:11)—a noble example, if we would imitate it; but we, I know not from what sloth, or rather contempt, receive the word of God in such a way that when we have learned three syllables, we immediately swell up with an opinion of wisdom, and think ourselves rich men and kings! Hence, you see so many who, unlearned themselves, keep tragically bawling out about the ignorance of the age! But what can you do? They are called, and would wish to be thought Christians, because they possess a slight knowledge of some commonplaces; and as they would be ashamed to be ignorant of anything, they with the greatest confidence, as if from a tripod, give forth decisions upon all things. Hence so many schisms, so many errors, so many stumbling blocks to our faith, through which the name and word of God are blasphemed among the ungodly. At length, (this is the head of the evil!) while they proceed obstinately to defend whatever they have once rashly babbled, they begin to consult the oracles of God, in order that they may there find support to their errors. Then—good God!—what do they not pervert, what do they not adulterate and corrupt, that they may, I do not say bend, but distort it to their own view? As was truly said by the poet, "Fury supplies armor."

Is this the way of learning: to roll the Scriptures over and over, and twist them about in search of something that may minister to our lust, or to force them into subjection to our sense? Nothing can be more absurd than this, O pernicious pest! O tares certainly sown by an enemy's hand, for the purpose of rendering the true seed useless! And do we still wonder at the many sects among those who had at first given in their adherence to the gospel and the reviving word? I, for my part, am terrified by the dreadful denunciation, "The kingdom of God shall be taken from you, and given to a nation bringing forth the fruits thereof" (Matt. 21:43).

Here, however, I desist from my complaints: for I should write a large volume were I to declaim in just terms on the perversity of this age. Let us, brethren, warned by so many examples, at length, though late, become wise. Let us always hang on our Lord's lips, and neither add to His wisdom nor mix up with it anything of our own, lest like leaven it corrupt the whole mass, and make even the very salt which is within us to be without savor. Let us show ourselves to be such disciples as our Lord wishes to have: poor, empty, and void of self-wisdom; eager to learn but knowing nothing, and even wishing to know nothing but what He has taught; shunning everything of foreign growth as the deadliest poison.

I would here obviate the objections of those who will blame my present undertaking, charging me with stirring up fierce contests about nothing, and making trifling differences the source of violent dissensions: for there are not wanting some who so reproach me. My answer is, that when Divine

Truth is avowedly attacked, we must not tolerate the adulteration of one single *iota* of it. It is certainly no trivial matter to see God's light extinguished by the devil's darkness; and besides, this matter is of greater moment than many suppose. Nor is it true as they allege that he who does not acquiesce in the errors of others, shows deadly hate by dissenting from them. I have censured the curiosity of those who would agitate questions which are truly nothing else than mere tortures to the intellect. But after they have stirred this *camarina*, their temerity must be repressed, lest it should prevail over the truth. Whether I have succeeded in this I know not: it was certainly my wish, and I have done the best I could. If others can do better, let them come forward for the public good!

Basel, 1536

Psychopannychia
THE SLEEP OF THE SOUL

In following out this discussion, I will not labor the matter much, but endeavor to explain myself with the greatest simplicity and clearness. In every discussion, indeed, it is of the greatest consequence that the subject be clearly seen by the writer, and laid distinctly before his readers; lest either he wander beyond his bounds, and lose himself in mere loquacity, or they, ignorant of the ground, go astray from not knowing the road. This is particularly necessary to be observed when the subject is matter of controversy, since there we do not merely propose to teach, but have to do with an opponent who (such is man's temper) certainly will not, if he can help it, allow himself to be vanquished, nor will confess defeat so long as he can sport and make a diversion by caviling rejoinders and tergiversation. The best method of pressing an enemy and holding him fast so that he cannot escape, is to exhibit the controverted point, and explain it so distinctly and clearly, that you can bring him at once as it were to close quarters.

Our controversy, then, relapses to the human soul. Some, while admitting it to have a real existence, imagine that it sleeps in a state of insensibility from death to the judgment day, when it will awake from its sleep; while others will sooner admit anything than its real existence, maintaining that it is merely a vital power which is derived from arterial spirit on the action of the lungs, and being unable to exist without body, perishes along with the body, and vanishes away and becomes evanescent till the period when the whole man shall be raised again.

We, on the other hand, maintain both that it is a substance, and after the death of the body truly lives, being endued both with sense and understanding. Both these points we undertake to prove by clear passages of Scripture. Here let human wisdom give place; for though it thinks much about the soul it perceives no certainty with regard to it. Here, too, let philosophers give place, since on almost all subjects their regular practice is to put neither end nor measure to their dissensions, while on this subject in particular they quarrel, so that you will scarcely find two of them agreed on any single point! Plato, in some passages, talks nobly of the faculties of the soul; and Aristotle, in discoursing of it, has surpassed all in acuteness. But what the soul is, and whence it is, it is vain to ask at them, or indeed at the whole body of sages, though they certainly thought more purely and wisely on the subject than some amongst ourselves, who boast that they are the disciples of Christ.

But before proceeding farther, we must cut off all handle for logomachy,[1] which might be furnished by our giving the name of "soul" and "spirit" indiscriminately to that which is the subject of controversy, and yet sometimes speaking of the two as different. By Scripture usage different meanings are given to these terms; and most people, without attending to this difference, take up the first meaning which occurs to them, keep fast hold of it, and pertinaciously maintain it. Others, having seen "soul" sometimes used for "life," hold this to be invariably the case, and will not allow themselves to be convinced of the contrary. If met with the passage from David, "Their soul will be blessed in life" (Psa. 49:19), they will interpret, that their life is blessed in life.

In like manner, if the passage from Samuel be produced, "By thy life, and by thy soul's life" (2 Sam. 11:11), they will say, that there is no meaning in these terms. We know that "soul" is very often used for *life* in such passages as the following: "My soul is in my hands" (Psa. 119:109); "Why do I tear my flesh with my teeth, and carry my soul in my hands?" (Job 13:14); "Is not the soul more than meat" (Matt. 6:25); "Thou fool, this night shall thy soul be required of thee"

---

[1] An argument about words.

(Luke 12:20). There are other similar passages which these soul-slayers always have in their mouth. There is no ground, however, for their great self-complacency, since they ought to observe that *soul* is there used metonymically[2] for *life*, because the soul is the cause of life, and life depends on the soul—a figure which boys learn even from their rudiments. It is impossible not to wonder at the presumption of these men, who have so high an opinion of themselves, and would gladly be thought wise by others, though they require to be taught the use of figures and the first elements of speech.

In this sense it was said that "the soul of Jonathan was knit to the soul of David" (1 Sam. 18:1); the soul of Sychem (Shechem) "clave unto Dinah the daughter of Jacob" (Gen. 34:3); and Luke says, that "the multitude of the believers was of one heart and soul" (Acts 4:32). Who sees not that there is much force in such Hebraisms as the following? "Bless the Lord, O my soul," (Psa. 103:1); "My soul doth magnify the Lord" (Psa. 104:1); "Say to my soul, I am thy salvation" (Luke 1:46). An indescribable something more is expressed

---

[2] "In rhetoric, a trope in which one word is put for another; a change of names which have some relation to each other; as when we say, 'a man keeps a good table.' instead of good provisions. 'We read Virgil.' that is, his poems or writings. 'They have Moses and the prophets,' that is, their books or writings. A man has a clear head, that is, understanding, intellect; a warm heart, that is affections."
—*American Dictionary of the English Language*, 1828.

than if it were said without addition, Bless the Lord; I magnify the Lord, Say to me, I am thy salvation!

Sometimes the word "soul" is used merely for a *living man*, as when sixty souls are said to have gone down into Egypt (Exod. 1:5). Again, "The soul that sinneth, it shall die" (Ezek. 28:4); "The soul which turneth aside to wizards and soothsayers shall die the death" (Lev. 20:6); etc. Sometimes also it is called the *breath* which men inhale and respire, and in which the vital motion of the body resides. In this sense I understand the following passages, "Anxiety seizes me though my whole soul is still in me" (2 Sam. 1:9); "His soul is in him" (Acts 20:10); "Let the soul of the child return within him" (1 Kgs. 17:21). Nay, in the very same sense in which we say, in ordinary language, that the soul is "breathed out" and "expires," Scripture speaks of the soul "departing," as when it is said of Rachel, "And when her soul was departing (for she died) she called the name of the child Benoni" (Gen. 35:18).

We know that spirit is *literally* "breath" and "wind," and for this reason is frequently called πνοὴν (*pnoēn*) by the Greeks. We know that it is used by Isaiah for a thing vain and worthless, "We have conceived and brought forth spirit," or "wind" (Isa. 26:18). It is very often taken for what is *regenerated* in us by the Spirit of God. For when Paul says that "the spirit lusteth against the flesh" (Gal. 5:17), he does not mean that the soul fights with the flesh, or reason with desire;

but that the soul itself, in as far as it is governed by the Spirit of God, wrestles with itself, though in as far as it is still devoid of the Spirit of God, it is subject to its lusts. We know that when the two terms are joined, "soul" means *will*, and "spirit" means *intellect*. Isaiah thus speaks, "My soul hath longed for thee in the night, but I will also wake to thee in my spirit, within me" (Isa. 26:9).

And when Paul prays that the Thessalonians may be entire in spirit, and soul, and body, so that they may be without blame at the coming of Jesus Christ (1 Thess. 5:23), his meaning is, that they may think and will all things rightly, and may not use their members as instruments of unrighteousness. To the same effect the Apostle elsewhere says, that the word of God is quick and piercing, like a two-edged sword, reaching to the division of soul and spirit, of the joints and marrow, and is a discerner of the thoughts of the heart (Heb. 4:12). In this last passage, however, some understand by "spirit" that reasoning and willing essence of which we now dispute; and by "soul," the vital motion and senses which philosophers call superior and inferior, *i.e.*, ὁρμαὶ καὶ αἰσθήσεις (*ormai kai aisthēseis*). But since in numerous passages both parties hold it to mean the immortal essence which is the cause of life in man, let them not raise disputes about mere names, but attend to the thing itself, by whatever name distinguished. How real it is let us now show.

And we will begin with man's creation, wherein we shall see of what nature he was made at first. The Sacred History tells us (Gen. 1:26) of the purpose of God, before man was created, to make him "after his own image and likeness." These expressions cannot possibly be understood of his body, in which, though the wonderful work of God appears more than in all other creatures, his image nowhere shines forth (Ambros. *lib.* 6, hex. August. cap. 4. *de Trinit. et alibi*).

For who is it that speaks thus, "Let us make man in our own image and likeness?" God himself, who is a Spirit, and cannot be represented by any bodily shape. But as a bodily image, which exhibits the external face, ought to express to the life all the traits and features, that thus the statue or picture may give an idea of all that may be seen in the original, so this image of God must, by its likeness, implant some knowledge of God in our minds. I hear that some triflers say that the image of God refers to the dominion which was given to man over the brutes, and that in this respect man has some resemblance to God, whose dominion is over all. Into this mistake even Chrysostom fell when he was carried away in the heat of debate against the insane Anthropomorphites. But Scripture does not allow its meaning to be thus evaded: for Moses, to prevent any one from placing this image in the flesh of man, first narrates that the body was formed out of clay, and makes no mention of the image of God; thereafter, he says, that "the breath of life" was introduced into this clay body, making the image of God not to become effulgent in man till he was complete in all his parts. What then, it will be asked, do you think that that breath of life is the image of God? No, indeed, although I might say so with many, and perhaps not improperly (Hilar. in Psalm 63; Aug. *Lib. de Spiritu et Anima*, cap. 39; Basil, hex. *Hom.* 8). For what if I should maintain that the distinction was constituted by the word of God, by which that breath of life is distinguished from the souls of brutes? For whence do the souls of other animals arise? God says, "Let the earth bring forth the living soul," etc. Let that which has sprung of earth be resolved into earth. But the soul of man is not of the earth. It was made by the mouth of the Lord, *i.e.*, by his secret power.

Here, however, I do not insist, lest it should become a ground of quarrel. All I wish to obtain is, that the image itself is separate from the flesh. Were it otherwise, there would be no great distinctions, in man from its being said that he was made *in the image of God*; and yet it is repeatedly brought forward in Scripture, and highly celebrated. For what occasion was there to introduce God as deliberating, and, as it were, making it a subject of consultation, whether he should make an ordinary creature? In regard to all these things, "He spoke, and it was done." When he comes to this image, as if he were about to give a singular manifestation, he calls in his wisdom and power, and meditates with himself before he puts his hand to the work. Were these figurative modes of expression which represent the Lord, ἀνθρωποπαθῶς (*anthrōpopathōs*, in a human manner), in adaptation to our feeble capacity, so anxiously employed by Moses for a thing of nought? Was it not rather to give an exalted idea of the image of God impressed on man? Not contented with saying it once, he repeats it again and again. Whatever philosophers or these dreamers may pretend, we hold that nothing can bear the image of God but spirit, since God is a Spirit.

Here we are not left to conjecture what resemblance this image bears to its archetype. We easily learn it from the Apostle (Col. 3:10). When he enjoins us to "put on the new man, which is renewed in knowledge after the image of him who created him," he clearly shows what this image is, or wherein it consists; as he also does when he says (Eph. 4:24), "Put on the new man, who has been created after God in knowledge and true holiness." When we would comprehend all these things, in one word we say, that man, in respect of spirit, was made partaker of the wisdom, justice, and goodness of God. This mode of expression was followed by two sacred writers. The one, in dividing man into two parts—*body*, taken from the earth, and *soul*, derived from the image of God—briefly comprehended what Moses had more fully expressed (Eccl. 17:1), "God created man, and made him after his own image."

The other, desiring to state exegetically how far the image of God extended, called man "inexterminable," because created in the image of God (Wisd. 2:23). I would not urge the authority of these writers strongly on our opponents, did they not allege them against us. Still they ought to have some weight, if not as canonical, at least as ancient pious writers strongly supported. But, leaving them, let us hold the image of God in man to be that which can only have its seat in the Spirit.

Let us now hear what *Scripture* more distinctly states concerning the soul. When Peter speaks of the salvation of the soul, and says that carnal lusts war against the soul (1 Pet. 1:9, 22); when he enjoins us to keep our souls chaste, and calls Christ the "Bishop of our souls" (2 Pet. 2:25), what could he mean but that there were souls which could be saved—which could be assailed by vicious desires—which could be kept chaste, and be ruled by Christ their Bishop? In the history of Job we read, "How much more those who dwell in houses of clay, and have a foundation of earth?" (4:19).

This, if you attend to it, you must see to apply to the soul, which dwells in a clay body. He did not call man a vessel of clay, but says that he inhabits a vessel of clay, as if the good part of man (which is the soul) were contained in that earthly abode. Thus Peter says, "I think it right, as long as I am in this tabernacle, to stir you up by way of remembrance, knowing that in a short time I must put off this my tabernacle" (1 Pet.

1:13). By this form of expression we might, if we are not very stupid, understand that there is something in a tabernacle, and something which is taken out of a tabernacle, or which, as he says, is to put off a tabernacle. The same manifest distinction between the flesh and the spirit is made by the author of the Epistle to the Hebrews, when he calls those by whom we were begotten the parents of one flesh; but says that there is one God, "the Father of spirits" (12:9). Shortly after, having called God the King of the heavenly Jerusalem, he subjoins that its citizens are angels and "the spirits of just men made perfect" (12:23).

Nor do I see how we can otherwise understand Paul, when he says, "Having, therefore, these promises, let us cleanse ourselves from all pollution of the flesh and spirit" (2 Cor. 7:1). For it is clear that he does not there make the comparison which he elsewhere frequently uses when he attributes defilement to the spirit, by which term, in other passages, he merely means purity.

I will add another passage, though I see that those who wish to cavil will immediately betake themselves to their glosses. The passage is 1 Corinthians 2:11: "Who of men knows the things of a man, save the spirit of man that is in him? so also no man knows the things of God, but the Spirit of God." He might have said, that man knows the things which are his; but he applied the name to that part in which the power of thinking and understanding resides. Also, when he said, "The Spirit of God bears witness with our spirit, that we are the sons of God" (Rom. 8:16), did he not use the same peculiarity of expression? But, might we not convince them by a single passage? We know how often our Savior condemned the error of the Sadducees, which partly consisted, as Luke states in the Acts in denying the existence of spirit. The words are, "The Sadducees say that there is no resurrection, neither angel nor spirit; but the Pharisees acknowledge all these" (23:8). I fear they will cavil, and say that the words must be understood of the Holy Spirit or of angels. But this objection is easily met. He both mentioned the angels separately; and it is certain that those Pharisees had no knowledge of the Holy Spirit. This will be still better understood by those who know Greek. Luke uses the term πνεῦμα without adding the article, which he certainly would have added had he been speaking of the Holy Spirit.

If this does not stop their mouths, I do not see by what argument they can either be led or drawn, unless they choose to say that the opinion of the Sadducees, in denying spirit, was not condemned, or that of the Pharisees, in asserting it, approved. This quibble is met by the very words of the Evangelist: for, after stating Paul's confession, "I am a Pharisee," he adds this opinion held by the Pharisees. We must therefore either say that Paul used a *crafty* and malicious *pretense* (this could not be—in a confession of faith!), or that he held with the Pharisees on the subject of spirit. But if we give credit to *History* (*Eccl. Hist.*, c. 4. cap. 13), this belief among the Apostles was as firm and certain as that of the resurrection of the dead, or any other leading article of our faith. It will not be out of place here to quote the words, of Polycarp, a man breathing the spirit of a martyr in all his words and actions (*Hist. Eccl.*, cap. 19), one who was a disciple of the Apostles, and so purely delivered what he heard from them to posterity, that he never allowed it to be in any degree adulterated. He, then, among many illustrious sayings which he uttered when brought to the stake, said, that on that day he was to appear before God in spirit. About the same time Melito, Bishop of Sardis (*Hist. Eccl.*, c. 24), a man of like integrity, wrote a treatise, *On Body and Soul*. Were it now extant, our present labor would be superfluous: and so much did this belief prevail in a better age, that Tertullian places it among the common and primary conceptions of the mind which are commonly apprehended by nature. (Tertull. *de Resurrect. Carnis.*)

* * *

Although several arguments have already been advanced which, if I mistake not, establish the point for which I contend, namely, that the spirit or soul of man is a substance distinct from the body, what is now to be added will make the point still more certain. For I come to the *second head*, which

I propose to discuss: *That the soul, after the death of the body, still survives, endued with sense and intellect.* And it is a mistake to suppose that I am here affirming anything else than THE IMMORTALITY OF THE SOUL. For those who admit that the soul lives, and yet deprive it of all sense, feign a soul which has none of the properties of soul, or dissever the soul from itself, seeing that its nature, without which it cannot possibly exist, is to move, to feel, to be vigorous, to understand. As Tertullian says, "The soul of the soul is perception" (*Lib. de Carne Christi*).

Let us now learn this *immortality* from Scripture. When Christ exhorts his followers not to fear those who can kill the body, but cannot kill the soul, but to fear him who, after he hath killed the body, is able to cast the soul into the fire of Gehenna (Matt. 10:28), does he not intimate that the soul survives death? Graciously, therefore, has the Lord acted towards us, in not leaving our souls to the disposal of those who make no scruple of butchering them, or at least attempt it, but without the ability to do so. Tyrants torture, maim, burn, scourge, and hang, but it is only the body! It is God alone who has power over the soul, and can send it into hell fire. Either, therefore, the soul survives the body, or it is false to say that tyrants have no power over the soul! I hear them reply, that the soul is indeed slain for the present when death is inflicted, but does not perish, inasmuch as it will be raised again. When they would escape in this way, they must grant that neither is the body slain, since it too will rise; and because both are preserved against the Day of Judgment, neither perishes! But the words of Christ admit that the body is killed, and testify at the same time that the soul is safe. This form of expression Christ uses when he says, "Destroy this temple, and in three days I will raise it up" (John 2:19). He was speaking of the temple of his body. In like manner he exempts it from their power, when, in dying, he commends it into his Father's hands, as Luke writes (23:4, 6), and David had foretold (Psa. 31:6). And Stephen, after his example, says "Lord Jesus, receive my spirit!" (Acts 7:59). Here they absurdly pretend that Christ commends his life to his Father, and Stephen his to Christ, to be kept against the day of Resurrection. But the words, especially those of Stephen, imply something very different from this. And the Evangelist adds, concerning Christ, that having bowed his head, he delivered his spirit (John 19:30). These words cannot refer to panting or action of the lungs.

Not less evidently does the Apostle Peter show that, after death, the soul both exists and lives, when he says that Christ preached to the spirits in prison, not merely forgiveness for salvation to the spirits of the righteous, but also confusion to the spirits of the wicked (1 Pet. 1:19). For so I interpret the passage, which has puzzled many minds; and I am confident that, under favorable auspices, I will make good my interpretation. For after he had spoken of the humiliation of the cross of Christ, and shown that all the righteous must be conformed to his image, he immediately thereafter, to prevent them from falling into despair, makes mention of the Resurrection, to teach them how their tribulations were to end. For he states that Christ did not fall under death, but, subduing it, came forth victorious. He indeed says in words, that he was "put to death in the flesh, but quickened by the Spirit" (1 Pet. 3:18), but just in the same sense in which Paul says that he suffered in the humiliation of the flesh, but was raised by the power of the Spirit. Now, in order that believers might understand that the power belongs to them also, he subjoins that Christ exerted this power in regard to others, and not only towards the living, but also towards the dead; and, moreover, not only towards his servants, but also towards unbelievers and the despisers of his grace.

Let us understand, moreover, that the sentence is defective, and wants one of its two members. Many examples of this occur in Scripture, especially when, as here, several sentiments are comprehended in one clause. And let no one wonder that the holy Patriarchs who waited for the redemption of Christ are shut up in prison. As they saw the light at a distance, under a cloud and shade (as those who see the feeble light of dawn or twilight), and had not yet an exhibition of the divine blessing in which they rested, he gave the name of prison to their expectancy.

The meaning of the Apostle will therefore be, that Christ in spirit preached to those other spirits who were in prison. In other words, that the virtue of the redemption obtained by Christ appeared and was exhibited to the spirits of the dead. Now, there is a want of the other member which related to the pious, who acknowledged and received this benefit; but it is complete in regard to unbelievers, who received this announcement to their confusion. For when they saw but one redemption, from which they were excluded, what could they do but despair? I hear our opponents muttering, and saying that this is a gloss of my own invention, and that such authority does not bind them. I have no wish to bind them to my authority, I only ask them whether or not the spirits shut up in prison are spirits? There is another clearer passage in the same writer, when he says that the gospel was preached to the dead, in order that they may be judged according to men in the flesh, but live according to God in the spirit (1 Pet. 4:6). You see how, while the flesh is delivered over to death, life is claimed for the spirit. A relation is expressed between life and death, and, by antithesis, the one dies and the other lives.

We learn the same thing from Solomon, when describing man's death, he makes a wide difference between the soul and the body. He says, "Until the dust return to the earth whence it was, and the spirit return to God who gave it" (Eccl. 12:7).

I am aware that they are little affected by this argument, because they say that life returns to God, who is the fountain of life; and this is all. But the words themselves proclaim that in this way violence is done to them, and it is therefore needless to refute a silly quibble, which is unworthy of being either heard or read. Even this must imply, according to them, that souls return to the fountain of life only by a dream! Corresponding to this is a passage in Esdras, a writer whom I would not oppose to them did they not greatly lean upon him. Let them then hear their own Esdras, "The earth will render up those things which sleep in it, and dwell in silence; and the storehouses will render up the souls which were committed to them" (4 Esd. 3:2). They triflingly allege that the "storehouses" are *Divine Providence*, and that "souls" are *thoughts*, so that the Book of Life is to exhibit thoughts in the presence of God. They evidently speak thus, merely because they are ashamed to be silent, and have nothing better to say. But if we may turn about the Scriptures in this way, everything may be perverted!

Here, however, though I have ample supplies, I will not produce anything of my own, since the writer defends himself from this misinterpretation. A little before he had said, "Did not the souls of these petition in their abodes, saying, How long do we hope this, O Lord? When will the harvest of our reward come?" (Esd. 4:3). What are these souls which petition and hope? Here, if they would escape, they must dig another burrow for themselves!

Let us come now to the history of the rich man and Lazarus, the latter of whom, after all the labors and toils of his mortal life are past, is at length carried into Abraham's bosom, while the former, having had his comforts here, now suffers torments. A great gulf is interposed between the joys of the one and the sufferings of the other. Are these mere dreams—the gates of ivory which the poets fable? To secure a means of escape, they make the history a parable, and say, that all which truth speaks concerning Abraham, the rich man and the poor man, is fiction. Such reverence do they pay to God and his word! Let them produce even one passage from Scripture where any one is called by name in a parable! What is meant by the words: "There was a poor man named Lazarus?" Either the Word of God must lie, or it is a true narrative.

This is observed by the ancient expounders of Scripture. Ambrose says it is a narrative rather than a parable, inasmuch as the name is added. Gregory takes the same view. Certainly Tertullian, Irenaeus, Origen, Cyprian and Jerome, speak of it as a history. Among these, Tertullian thinks that, in the person of the rich man, Herod is designated, and in Lazarus, John the Baptist (Tertull. lib. *adv. Marcion*). The words of Irenaeus are these: "The Lord did not tell us a fable in the case of the rich man and Lazarus," etc. (Iren. lib. 4. *contra haeres*, cap. 4; Origen, *Hom.* 5 in Ezech.; Cyprian *epist.*, 3; Hieron. in Jes. c. 49 and 65; Hilar. in Psalm 3). And Cyril, in replying to the Arians, who drew from it an argument against the Divinity of Christ, does not relate it as a parable, but expounds it as a history (Cyril in John 1 chapter 22). They are more absurd when they bring forward the name of Augustine, pretending that he held their view. They affirm this, I presume, because in one place he says, "In the parable, by Lazarus is to be understood Christ, and by the rich man the Pharisees" (August. *de Genes. ad Liter.* lib. 8); when all he means is, that the narrative is converted into a parable if the person of Lazarus is assigned to Christ, and that of the rich man to the Pharisees. This is the usual custom with those who take up a violent prejudice in favor of an opinion. Seeing that they have no ground to stand upon, they lay hold not only of syllables but letters to twist them to their use! To prevent them from insisting here, the writer himself elsewhere declares, that he understands it to be a history. Let them now go and try to put out the light of day by means of their smoke!

They cannot escape without always falling into the same net: for though we should grant it to be a parable (this they cannot at all prove), what more can they make of it than just that there is a comparison which must be founded in truth? If these great theologians do not know this, let them learn it from their grammars, there they will find that a parable is a similitude, founded on reality. Thus, when it is said that a certain man had two sons to whom he divided his goods, there must be in the nature of things both a man and sons, inheritance and goods. In short, the invariable rule in parables is, that we first conceive a simple subject and set it forth; then, from that conception, we are guided to the scope of the parable—in other words, to the thing itself to which it is accommodated. Let them imitate Chrysostom, who is their Achilles in this matter. He thought that it was a parable, though he often extracts a reality from it, as when he proves from it that the dead have certain abodes, and shows the dreadful nature of Gehenna, and the destructive effects of luxury (Chrysos. *Hom.* 25 in Matt. *Hom.* 57; *in eundem, In Par ad The. Lapsor. Hom.* 4 Matt.). Not to lose many words here, let them consult common sense, if they have any, and they will easily perceive the nature and force of the parable.

* * *

Feeling desirous, as far as we can, to satisfy all, we will here say something respecting *the rest of the soul when, in sure trust in the divine promise, it is freed from the body*. Scripture, by the "bosom of Abraham," only means to designate this rest. *First*, we give the name of "rest" to that which our opponents call "sleep." We have no aversion, indeed, to the term *sleep*, were it not corrupted and almost polluted by their falsehoods. *Secondly*, by "rest" we understand, not sloth, or lethargy, or anything like the drowsiness of ebriety which they attribute to the soul; but tranquility of conscience and security, which always accompanies faith, but is never complete in all its parts till after death.

The Church, indeed, while still dwelling on the earth as a stranger, learns the blessedness of believers from the lips of the Lord: "My people will walk in the beauty of peace, and in the tents of trust, and in rich rest" (Isa. 32:18). She herself, on the other hand, giving thanks, sings to the Lord while blessing her: "O Lord, thou wilt give us peace: for thou hast performed all our works for us" (Isa. 26:12).

Believers have this *peace* on receiving the gospel, when they see that God, whom they dreaded as their Judge, has become their Father; themselves, instead of children of wrath, children of grace; and the bowels of the divine mercy poured out toward them, so that now they expect from God nothing but goodness and mildness. But since human life on earth is a warfare (Job 7:1), those who feel both the stings of sin and the remains of the flesh, must feel depression in the world, though with consolation in God—such consolation, however, as does not leave the mind perfectly calm and undisturbed. But when they shall be divested of flesh and the desires of the flesh (which, like domestic enemies, break their peace), then at length will they rest and recline with God: For thus speaks the Prophet:

> The just perisheth, and no man layeth it to heart; and men of mercy are gathered: for the just is gathered from the face of wickedness. Let peace come, let him who hath walked under his direction rest in his bed (Isa. 57:1).

Does he not call those to peace who had been the sons of peace? Still, as their peace was with God, and they had war in the world, he calls them to a higher degree of peace.

Accordingly, Ezekiel and John, when they would describe the throne of God's glory, encircle it with a rainbow, which we know to be the sign of the covenant between God and men. This John has taught more clearly in another passage, "Blessed are the dead who die in the Lord, yea, says the Scripture, that they may rest from their labors" (Ezek. 1:28; Rev. 9:3; 14:13).

This, then, is the bosom of Abraham: for it was he himself who, with ready mind, embraced the promises made to his own seed, never doubting that the word of God was efficacious and true: and as if God had actually performed what he had promised, he waited for that blessed seed with no less assurance than if he had had it in his hands, and perceived it with all his senses. Accordingly, our Lord bore this testimony to him, that "he saw His day and was glad" (John 8:56). Here is the peace of Abraham, here his rest, here his sleep; only let not an honorable name be polluted by the lips of these dull sleepers: for in what can *conscience* rest more pleasantly than in this peace, which opens to it the treasures of heavenly grace and intoxicates it with the sweetness of the Lord's cup? Why, O sleepers!, when you hear of intoxication, do you not think of vertigo, of heaviness, of your gross carnal sleep? Such are the inconveniences which ensue upon intoxication! Such may be your gross imaginations; but those who are taught of God understand that "sleep" is used, in this way, for the *peace of conscience* which the Lord bestows upon his followers in the abode of peace, and "intoxication" for the riches with which God satisfies his people in the abode of opulence. If Abraham possessed this peace when exposed to inroads from his enemies, to labors and dangers, nay, when bearing about with him his flesh, a domestic enemy than whom there is none more pernicious, how great must his peace be now that he has escaped from all hostile blows and darts?

No one can now wonder why the elect of God are said to "rest in the bosom of Abraham," when they have passed from this life to their God! It is just because they are admitted with Abraham, the father of the faithful, where they enjoy God fully without weariness. Wherefore, not without reason, Augustine says in a certain place, "As we call eternal life, so we may also call peace 'The end of the blessed:' for He can give nothing better who can give nothing greater or better than himself, being THE GOD OF PEACE" (August. *de Civit.* lib. 19).

Henceforth, when the "bosom of Abraham" is spoken of, let them not wrest it to their dream, since the truth of Scripture at once establishes and condemns their vanity. There is, I say, a rest, a heavenly Jerusalem, *i.e.,* a vision of peace, in which the God of peace gives himself to be seen by his peace-makers, according to the promise of Christ. How often does the Spirit make mention of this *peace* in Scripture, and use the figure of "sleeping" and "resting" so familiarly, that the use of no figure is more frequent! "Thy saints," says David, "will exult, they will rejoice in their beds" (Psa. 149:5; Isa. 57:2). Another says, "Thy dead shall live, thy slain shall rise again. Awake, and praise, ye dwellers in the dust, because thy dew is the dew of meadows, and thou shalt bring the land of giants to destruction" (1 Cor. 15:12; 1 Thess. 5:13; Matt. 5:8–9). "Go, my people, enter into thy tabernacles, shut thy doors upon thee, hide thyself for a little, until the indignation be overpast" (Isa. 26:19–20). Nay, the Hebrew tongue uses the word to signify any security and confidence. David, on the other hand, says, "I will sleep, and rest in peace" (Psa. 4:9) And the Prophet says,

> I will make a covenant, in that day, with the beast of the field, and with the bird of the air, and with the reptile of the earth; I will break the bow and the

sword, and banish war from the earth, and make them to sleep without terror (Hos. 2:18).

And Moses says, "I will give peace in your borders, and not one shall be afraid" (Lev. 26:6). And in the book of Job it is said,

> "Thou shalt have confidence in the hope set before thee, and buried wilt sleep secure. Thou shalt rest, and there will be none to terrify thee, and very many will supplicate thy face" (Job 11:18–19).

Of the same thing we are admonished by the Latin proverb, of "sleeping on both ears," meaning to live securely. The souls of the living, therefore, who rest in the word of the Lord, and desire not to anticipate the will of their God, but are ready to follow wherever he may invite, keep themselves under his hand, sleep, and have peace. The command given to them is, "If His truth tarry, wait for it" (Hab. 2:3). And again, "In hope and silence will be your strength" (Isa. 30:15).

Now, when they wait for something which they see not, and desire what they have not, it is evident that their peace is imperfect. On the other hand, while they confidently expect what they do expect, and in faith desire what they desire, it is clear that their desire is tranquil. This peace is increased and advanced by death, which, freeing, and as it were discharging them from the warfare of this world, leads them into the place of peace, where, while wholly intent on beholding God, they have nothing better to which they can turn their eyes or direct their desire. Still, something is wanting which they desire to see, namely, the complete and perfect glory of God, to which they always aspire. Though there is no impatience in their desire, their rest is not yet full and perfect, since he is said to rest who is where he desires to be; and the measure of desire has no end till it has arrived where it was tending. But if the eyes of the elect look to the supreme glory of God as their final good, their desire is always moving onward till the glory of God is complete, and this completion awaits the judgment day. Then will be verified the saying, "I will be satisfied, when I awake, with beholding thy countenance" (Psa. 17:15).

* * *

Not to omit the reprobate, whose doom need not give us great concern, I would like our opponents candidly to tell me, on what ground they have any hope of resurrection, unless it be because Christ rose? He is the first-begotten of the dead, and the first-fruits of them that rise again. As he died and rose again, so do we also die and rise again. For if the death to which we were liable was to be overcome by death, he undoubtedly suffered the same death as we do, and likewise in death suffered what we suffer. Scripture makes this plain when it calls him the first-begotten of the dead, and the firstfruits of them that rise again (Col. 1:18). And it thus teaches, that believers in the midst of death acknowledge him as their leader, and while they behold their death sanctified by his death, have no dread of its curse. This Paul intimates when he says, that he was made conformable to his death, until he should attain to the resurrection of the dead (Phil. 2:20). This conformity, here begun by the cross, he followed out until he should complete it by death.

Now, O dreamy sleepers, commune with your own hearts, and consider how Christ died. Did he sleep when he was working for your salvation? Not thus does he say of himself, "As the Father hath life in himself, so hath he given to the Son to have life in himself" (John 5:26). How could he who has life in himself lose it?

Let them not tell me that these things belong to his Divinity. For if there has been given to him who has not, it has been given to man and not to God to have life in himself. For seeing that Jesus Christ is Son of God and man, that which he is by nature as God is he also by grace as man, that thus we may all receive of his fullness, and grace for grace. When men hear that there is life with God, what hope can they conceive from it, while they at the same time know that by their sins; a cloud is interposed between them and God? But it is surely great consolation to know that God the Father has anointed Christ with the oil of joy above his fellows—that the man Christ has received from the Father gifts for men, so that we may be able to find life in our nature. Hence we read that the multitude, after the boy was raised, glorified God who had given such power to men (Acts 20:12). This was certainly seen by Cyril, who agrees with us in the exposition of this passage. But when we say that Christ, as man, has life in himself, we do not say that he is the cause of life to himself.

This may be made plain from a familiar comparison. A fountain from which all drink, and from which streams flow and are derived, is said to have water in itself; and yet it has it not of itself but of the source, which constantly supplies what may suffice both for the running streams and the men who drink of it. Accordingly, Christ has life in himself, *i.e.*, fullness of life, by which he both himself lives and quickens others; yet he has it not of himself, as he elsewhere declares that he lives by the Father. And though as God he had life in himself, yet when he assumed human nature, he received from the Father the gift of having life in himself in that nature also. These things give us the fullest assurance that Christ could not be extinguished by death, even in respect of his human nature; and that although he was truly and naturally delivered to the death which we all undergo, he, however, always retained the gift of the Father. Indeed, death was a separation of soul and body. But the soul never lost its life. Having been commended to the Father it could not but be safe.

This is intimated by the words in Peter's sermon, in which he affirms that it was impossible he could be holden of death, in order that the Scripture might be fulfilled, "Thou wilt not leave my soul in hell, nor allow thy Holy One to see corruption" (Acts 2:27).

Though we should grant that in this prophecy "soul" is used for life, Christ asks and expects two things of his Father—not to abandon his soul to perdition, nor allow himself to be subjected to corruption. This was fulfilled. For his soul was supported by divine power, and did not fall into perdition, and the body was preserved in the tomb till its resurrection. All these things Peter embraced in one expression, when he says that Christ could not be held of death κρατεῖσθαι, *i.e.*, yield to the domination, or fall under the power of death, or continue to be seized by it. It is true that Peter, in that discourse, leaving off the consideration of the soul, continues to speak of the incorruption of the body only. This he does to convince the Jews, on the authority of their own writers, that this prophecy did not apply to David, whose sepulcher was extant among them, whose body they knew to have fallen under corruption, so that they could not deny the resurrection of our Lord. Another proof of the immortality of his soul was given us by our Savior, when he made the confinement of Jonah three days within the whale's belly to be a type of his death, stating that thus he would be three days and three nights in the belly of the earth. But Jonah cried unto the Lord from the belly of the fish, and was heard. That belly is death. He therefore had his soul safe in death, and by means of it could cry unto the Lord.

Isaac, also, who was a type of Christ, and was restored to his father from death, by a kind of type of the resurrection, as the Apostle says, shows us the truth in a figure. For after having been bound, and placed upon the altar as a prepared victim, he was loosed by the order of God. But the ram which had been caught in the thicket was substituted for Isaac. And why is it that Isaac does not die, but just because Christ has given immortality to that which is peculiar to man—I mean the soul? But the ram, the irrational animal which is given up to death in his stead, is the body. In the binding of Isaac is represented the soul, which showed only a semblance of dying in the death of Christ, and the same is daily exhibited in ordinary instances of death. But as the soul of Christ was set free from prison, so our souls also are set free before they perish. Let any one of you now put on a supercilious air, and pretend that the death of Christ was a sleep—or let him go over and join the camp of Apollinaris! Christ was indeed awake when he exerted himself for your salvation; but you sleep your sleep, and, buried in the darkness of blindness, give no heed to his wakening calls!

Besides, it not only consoles us to think that Christ, our Head, did not perish in the shadow of death, but we have the additional security of his resurrection, by which he constituted himself the Lord of death, and raised all of us who have any part in him above death, so that Paul did not hesitate to say, that "our life is hid with Christ in God" (Col. 3:3). Elsewhere he says, "I live, yet not I, but; Christ liveth in me" (Gal. 2:20). What remains for our opponents but to cry with open mouth that Christ sleeps in sleeping souls? For if Christ lives in them he also dies in them. If, therefore, the life of Christ is ours, let him who insists that our life is ended by death pull Christ down from the right hand of the Father and consign him to the second death. If he can die, our death is certain; if he has no end of life, neither can our souls ingrafted in him be ended by any death!

But why labor the point? Is there any obscurity in the words, "Because I live, ye shall live also" (John 14:19)? If we live because he lives, then if we die he does not live. Is there any obscurity in his promise, that he will remain in all who are united to him by faith, and they in him (John 6:56)? Therefore, if we would deprive the members of life, let us dissever them from Christ. Our confession, which is sufficiently established, is this, "In Adam all die, but in Christ are made alive" (1 Cor 15:22).

These things are splendidly and magnificently handled by Paul. "If the Spirit of Christ dwell in us, the body is dead because of sin, but the Spirit is life because of righteousness" (Rom. 8:10). He no doubt calls the body the mass of sin, which resides in man from the native property of the flesh; and the spirit the part of man spiritually regenerated. Wherefore, when a little before he deplored his wretchedness because of the remains of sin adhering to him (Rom. 7:24) he did not desire to be taken away altogether, or to be nothing, in order that he might escape from that misery, but to be freed from the body of death, *i.e.*, that the mass of sin in him might die, that the spirit, being purged, and, as it were, freed from dregs, he might have peace with God through this very circumstance; declaring, that his better part was held captive by bodily chains and would be freed by death.

I wish we could with true faith perceive of what nature the kingdom of God is which exists in believers, even while they are in this life. For it would at the same time be easy to understand that eternal life is begun. He who cannot deceive promised thus: "Whoso hears my words has eternal life, and does not come into condemnation, but hath passed from death unto life" (John 5:24).

If an entrance has been given into eternal life, why do they interrupt it by death? Elsewhere he says, "This is the work of the Father, that every one who believes in the Son may not perish, but have eternal life; and I will raise him up at the last day" (John 6:40).

Again,

> He who eats my flesh, and drinks my blood, hath eternal life; and I will raise him up at the last day. Not as your fathers did eat manna in the wilderness and are dead. He who eateth of this bread shall live for ever" (John 6:54).

Do not attempt here to introduce your fictitious comments concerning the Last Day. He promises us two things: eternal life and the resurrection. Though you are told of two you admit only one! Another expression of Christ is still more decisive. He says, "I am the resurrection and the life. He who believeth on me shall live though he were dead. And whoso liveth and believeth in me shall not die for ever" (John 11:25–26).

It will not do to say, that those who are raised do not die for ever. Our Lord meant not only this, but that it is impossible they can ever die. This meaning is better expressed by the Greek words εἰς τὸν αἰῶνα (*eis ton aiōna*) equivalent in Latin to *in seculum*: for when we say that a thing will not be *in seculum*, we affirm that it will never be at all. Thus in another passage, "Whoso will keep my word shall not see death for ever" (John 8:51). This invincibly proves, that he who will keep the word of the Lord shall not see death; and it should be sufficient to arm the faith of Christians against the perverseness of these men. This is our belief, this our expectation. Meanwhile, what remains for them but to continue sleeping on till they are awakened by the clang of the trumpet which shall break their slumbers like a thief in the night?

And if God is the life of the soul, just as the soul is the life of the body, how can it be that the soul keeps acting upon the body so long as it is in the body, and never is for an instant idle, and yet that God should cease from acting as if he were fatigued! If such is the vigor of the soul in sustaining, moving, and impelling a lump of clay, how great must be the energy of God in moving and actuating the soul to which agility is natural! Some go the length of saying, that the soul becomes evanescent; others, that its vigor is not exercised after the fetters of the body are dissolved. What answer then will they give to David's hymn (Psa. 73) wherein he describes the beginning, middle, and end of the life of the blessed? He says, "They will go from strength to strength; the Lord of hosts will be seen in Zion;" or, as the Hebrew has it, *from abundance to abundance*. If they always increase till they see God, and pass from that increase to the vision of God, on what ground do these men bury them in drunken slumber and deep sloth?

The same thing is testified still more clearly by the Apostle when he says, that if they are dissolved they are no longer able to resist the Spirit of God. His words are,

> We know that if the earthly house of this tabernacle were dissolved, we have a building of God, a house

not made with hands, eternal in the heavens. For in this we groan, desiring to be clothed upon with our house which is from heaven; if so be that being clothed we shall not be found naked. For we who are in this tabernacle do groan being burdened, not because we wish to be unclothed, but clothed upon, that mortality may be swallowed up of life" (2 Cor. 5:1–3).

A little afterwards he says,

> Therefore we are always of good courage, and know that while we are at home in the body we are absent from the Lord; (for we walk by faith, not by sight;) we are confident, and would rather be absent from the body and present with the Lord (2 Cor. 5:6–8).

Here the evasion they have recourse to is, that the Apostle's words refer to the Day of Judgment, when both we shall be clothed upon, and mortality shall be swallowed up of life. Accordingly, they say, the Apostle includes both in one paragraph: "We must all appear before the judgment-seat of Christ" (2 Cor. 5:10).

But why do they refer this clothing upon to the body, rather than to spiritual blessings with which we are richly supplied at death? What forces them to interpret the life there spoken of as meaning *resurrection*? The simple and obvious meaning of the Apostle is, we desire indeed to depart from this prison of the body, but not to wander uncertain without a home: There is a better home which the Lord has prepared for us; clothed with it, we shall not be found naked. Christ is our clothing, and our armor is that which the Apostle puts upon us (Eph. 6:11). And it is written, "The king will admire the beauty of his spouse, who will be richly provided with gifts, and all glorious within" (Psa. 45:13). In summary, the Lord has put a seal upon his own people, whom he will acknowledge both at death and at the resurrection (Rev. 7). Why do they not rather look back to what he had just said in the previous context with which he connects this very sentence? "Though our outward man decays, our inward man is renewed day by day" (2 Cor. 4:16).

They find it more difficult to evade what the Apostle subjoins as to our appearance before the judgment-seat of Christ, after having said, that whether at home or living abroad we labor to please him. Since by *home* he means the body, what are we to understand by this *living abroad?*

Therefore, though we were not to add one word, the meaning is obvious without an interpreter. It is, that both in the body and out of the body we labor to please the Lord; and that we shall perceive the presence of God when we shall be separated from this body—that we will no longer walk by faith but by sight, since the load of clay by which we are pressed down, acts as a kind of wall of partition, keeping us far away from God. Those triflers, on the contrary, absurdly pretend that at death we are to be more widely separated from God than we are during life! In regard even to the present life, it is said of the righteous, "They shall walk, O Lord, in the light of thy countenance" (Psa. 88); and again, "The Spirit himself beareth witness with our spirit that we are the children of God" (Rom. 8:16); besides many other passages to the same effect. But these men deprive the righteous at death both of the light of God's countenance and the witness of his Spirit; and, therefore, if they are correct, we are happier now than we are to be at death! For, as Paul says in Philippians 3, even while we live under the elements of this world, we have a habitation and citizenship in the heavens. But if, as they maintain, our souls are at death overwhelmed with lethargy, and buried in oblivion, they must lose every kind of spiritual enjoyment which they previously possessed.

We are better taught by the Sacred Writings. The body, which decays, weighs down the soul, and confining it within an earthly habitation, greatly limits its perceptions. If the body is the prison of the soul, if the earthly habitation is a kind of fetters, what is the state of the soul when set free from this prison, when loosed from these fetters? Is it not restored to itself, and as it were made complete, so that we may truly say, that all which it gains is so much lost to the body? Whether they will or not, they must be forced to confess, that when we put off the load of the body, the war between the spirit and the flesh ceases. In short, the mortification of the flesh is the quickening of the spirit. Then the soul, set free from impurities, is truly spiritual, so as to be in accordance with the will of God, and not subject to the tyranny of the flesh, rebelling against it. In short, the mortification of the flesh will be the quickening of the spirit: For then the soul, having shaken off all kinds of pollution, is truly spiritual, so that it consents to the will of God, and is no longer subjected to the tyranny of the flesh; thus dwelling in tranquility, with all its thoughts fixed on God. Are we to say that it sleeps, when it can rise aloft unencumbered with any load? That it slumbers, when it can perceive many things by sense and thought, no obstacle preventing? These things not only manifest the errors of these men, but also their malignant hostility to the works and operations which the Scriptures proclaim that God performs in his saints.

We acknowledge God as growing in his elect, and increasing from day to day. This the wise man teaches us, when he says, "The path of the just is as the light, increasing into the perfect day" (Prov. 4:18). And the Apostle affirms, that "He who has begun a good work in you will perfect it against the day of the Lord Jesus" (Phil. 1:6).

These men not only intermit the work of God for a time, but even extinguish it. Those who formerly went from faith to faith, from virtue to virtue, and enjoyed a foretaste of blessedness when they exercised themselves in thinking of

God, they deprive both of faith and virtue, and all thought of God, and merely place on beds, in a sluggish and lethargic state! For how do they interpret that progress? Do they think that souls are perfected when they are made heavy with sleep as a preparation for their being brought sleek and fat into the presence of God when he shall sit in judgment? Had they a particle of sense they would not prattle thus absurdly about the soul, but would make all the difference between a celestial soul and an earthly body, that there is between heaven and earth. When the Apostle longs to depart and to be with Christ (Phil. 1:23), do they think he wishes to fall asleep so as no longer to feel any desire of Christ? Was this all he was longing for when he said he knew he had a building of God, a house not made with hands, as soon as the earthly house of his tabernacle should be dissolved? (2 Cor. 5:1). Where were the benefit of being with Christ were he to cease to live the life of Christ?

What! Are they not overawed by the words of the Lord when, calling himself the God of Abraham, Isaac, and Jacob, he says, he is "God not of the dead but of the living?" (Matt. 22:32).

Is he, then, neither to be to them a God, nor are they to be to him a people? (Mark 12:27). But they say that these things will be realized when the dead shall be raised to life. Although the question expressly asked is, Have you not read what was said concerning the resurrection of the dead? This evasion will not serve their purpose. Christ having to do with the Sadducees, who denied not only the resurrection of the dead but the immortality of the soul, convicts them of two errors by this single expression. For if God is God not of the dead but of the living, and Abraham, Isaac, and Jacob had departed this life when God spoke to Moses calling himself their God, the inference is, that they were living another life.

Those must surely be in being of whom God says that he is their God. Hence Luke adds, "For all things live to him" (Luke 30:28), not meaning that all things live by the presence of God, but by his energy. It follows, therefore, that Abraham, Isaac, and Jacob are alive. To this passage we add that of the Apostle, "Whether we live, we live unto the Lord, whether we die, we die unto the Lord: whether we live or die, we are the Lord's. For, for this Christ both died and rose again, that he might be Lord of the living and the dead" (Rom. 14:8–9). What more solid foundation could there be on which to rear our faith, than to say that Christ rules over the dead? There can only be rule over persons who exist, the exercise of government necessarily implying the existence of subjects.

Testimony is also borne against them in heaven before God and his angels, by the souls of the martyrs under the altar, who with loud voice cry,

> How long, O Lord, dost thou not avenge our blood on those who dwell on the earth? And there were

> given unto them white robes, and it was told them still to rest for a season, until the number of their fellow-servants and their brethren who were to be slain like them should be completed (Rev. 6:10–11).

The souls of the dead cry aloud, and white robes are given unto them! O sleeping spirits! What are white robes to you? Are they pillows on which you are to lie down and sleep? You see that white robes are not at all adapted for sleep, and therefore, when thus clothed, they must be awake. If this is true, these white robes undoubtedly designate the commencement of glory, which the Divine liberality bestows upon martyrs while waiting for the Day of Judgment.

It is no new thing for Scripture to designate glory, festivity, and joy, under the figure of a white robe. It was in a white robe the Lord appeared in vision to Daniel. In this garb the Lord was seen on Mount Tabor. The angel of the Lord appeared to the women at the sepulcher in white raiment (Dan. 7:9; Matt. 17:2; Mark 16:5); and under the same form did the angels appear to the disciples as they continued gazing up to heaven after their Lord's ascension (Matt 28:3; Acts 1:10). In the same, too, did the angel appear to Cornelius (Acts 10:30), and when the son who had wasted his substance had returned to his father, he was clothed in the best robe, as a symbol of joy and festivity (Luke 15:22).

Again, if the souls of the dead cried aloud, they were not sleeping. When, then, did that drowsiness overtake them? Let no one here obtrude the expression that "the blood of Abel cried for vengeance!" I am perfectly ready to admit that when blood has been shed, it is an ordinary figure to represent it as calling aloud for vengeance. In this passage, however, it is certain that the feeling of the martyrs is represented to us by crying, because their desire is expressed and their petition described without any figure, "How long, O Lord, dost thou not avenge?" etc. Accordingly, in the same book John has described a twofold resurrection as well as a twofold death; namely, one of the soul before judgment, and another when the body will be raised up, and when the soul also will be raised up to glory. "Blessed," says he, "are those who have part in the first resurrection; on them the second death takes no effect" (Rev. 20:6). Well, then, may you be afraid who refuse to acknowledge that first resurrection, which, however, is the only entrance to beatific glory.

One of the most fatal blows to the dogma of these men is the answer which was given to the thief who implored mercy. He prayed, "Lord, remember me when thou comest to thy kingdom;" and he hears the reply, "Today shalt thou be with me in paradise" (Luke 22:42). He who is everywhere, promises that he will be present with the thief. And he promises paradise, because he who thus enjoys God has fullness of delight. Nor does he put him off for a long series of days. He calls him to the joys of his kingdom on that very day! They endeavor to evade the force of our Savior's expression by a paltry quibble. They say, "One day is with him as a thousand years" (2 Pet. 3:8). But they remember not that God in speaking to man, accommodates himself to human sense. They are not told that in Scripture one day is used for a thousand years. Who would listen to the expounder, who, on being told that God would do something today, should immediately explain it as meaning thousands of years? When Jonah declared to the Ninevites, "Forty days and Nineveh shall be destroyed" (Jonah 3:4), might they have waited securely for the future judgment, as not to be inflicted till forty thousand years should have elapsed? It was not in this sense Peter said, that in the sight of God a thousand years were as one day; but when some false prophets counted days and hours for the purpose of charging God with falsehood in not fulfilling His promises, the moment they wished for it, he reminds them that with God is eternity, compared with which a thousand years are scarcely a single moment.

Feeling themselves completely entangled, they maintain that in Scripture *today* means the duration of the New, and *yesterday* the duration of the Old Testament! To this meaning they wrest the passage "Jesus Christ, yesterday, and today, the same for ever" (Heb. 13:8). Here they are totally in error. For, if he was only *yesterday*, then not being before the commencement of the Old Testament, he might at one time have begun to be! Where then will be Jesus, the eternal God, in respect of humanity, even the first-born of every creature, and the Lamb slain from the foundation of the world? (Col. 1:15; Rev. 13:8). Again, if *today* means the time which intervenes between the incarnation of Christ and the day of judgment, we hold that paradise will be enjoyed by the thief previous to the period at which they say that souls are awakened out of sleep! Thus, then, they will be forced to confess that the promise given to the thief was fulfilled before the judgment, though they at the same time insist that it was not to be fulfilled till after the judgment. But if they confine the expression to the time which follows the judgment, why does the author of the Epistle add "*For ever?*" And to make their darkness visible, if Christ referred in that promise to the period of judgment, he ought not to have said *today*, but at a future age; just as Isaiah, when he wished to express the mystery of the resurrection, called Christ "the Father of the future age" (Isa. 9:6).

But since the Apostle used the expression, "Yesterday, today, and for ever," for what we are accustomed to express by "Was, is, and shall be"—the three tenses being with us equivalent to eternity—what more do they by their quibble than pervert the Apostle's meaning? That the term *yesterday* is used to comprehend an eternal duration may be distinctly learned from the Prophet, who writes, "Tophet has been ordained for the wicked from the time of yesterday" (Isa. 30:33), while we know from the words of Christ that fire has been prepared from eternity for the devil and his angels (Matt. 25:41). All of them who have any judgment or sound mind, here see that they have no means left by which they can elude the truth made thus manifest. Still, however, they continue to cavil and say, that paradise was promised to the thief on that day, just as death was denounced to our first parents on the day on which they should taste of the tree of the knowledge of good and evil. Were we to grant this, we can still force them to admit that the robber on that day was restored from the misery into which Adam fell on the day on which he transgressed the law that had been laid upon him. Moreover, when I shall finally discourse of death, I shall make it abundantly plain, if I mistake not, how our parents did die on the day on which they rebelled against God.

* * *

Let me now direct my discourse to those who with a pure conscience, remembering the promises of God, acquiesce in them. Brethren, let no man rob you of this faith, though all the gates of hell should resist, since you have the assurance of God, who cannot deny his truth! There is not the least obscurity in his language to the Church, while still a pilgrim on the earth: "You shall no more have the sun to shine by day, nor shall the moon illumine you by her brightness, for the Lord shall be your everlasting light" (Isa. 60:19).

Here if they, after their usual custom, refer us to the last resurrection, it will be easy to refute the absurdity from individual expressions of the chapter, in which the Lord at one time promises his Messiah, and at another promises to admit the Gentiles to alliance, etc. Let us ever call to mind what the Spirit hath taught by the mouth of David:

> "The just shall flourish like the palm-tree, he shall be multiplied like the cedar on Lebanon. Those who have been planted in the house of the Lord will flourish in the courts of our God, they will still bud forth in their old age, they will be fat and flourishing" (Psa. 92:13).

Be not alarmed because all the powers of nature are thought to fail at the very time when you hear of a budding and flourishing old age. Reflecting with yourselves on these things, let your souls, in unison with David's, exclaim, "O my soul, bless the Lord, who satisfieth thy mouth with good: thy youth shall be renewed like the eagle's" (Psa. 103:5). Leave the rest to the Lord, who guards our entrance and our exit from this time forth even for evermore. He it is who sendeth the early and the latter rain upon his elect. Of him we have been told, "Our God is the God of salvation," and "to the Lord our God belong the issues of death" (Psa. 68:20).

Christ expounded this goodness of the Father to us when he said, "Father, with regard to those whom thou hast given me, I will that where I am they also may be with me, that they may behold my glory which thou hast given me" (John 17:24).

The faith thus sustained by all prophecies, evangelical truth, and Christ himself, let us hold fast—the faith that our spirit is the image of God, like whom it lives, understands, and is eternal. As long as it is in the body it exerts its own powers; but when it quits this prison-house it returns to God, whose presence, it meanwhile enjoys while it rests in the hope of a blessed resurrection. This rest is its paradise. On the other hand, the spirit of the reprobate, while it waits for the dreadful judgment, is tortured by that anticipation, which the Apostle for that reason calls φοβεράν (*phoberan*, fearful). To inquire beyond this is to plunge into the abyss of the Divine mysteries. It is enough to have learned what the Spirit, our best Teacher, deemed it sufficient to have taught. His words are, "Hear me, and your soul shall live" (Isa. 4:8).

How wisely, in opposition to the vanity and arrogance of those men, was it said, "The souls of the righteous are in the hands of God, and the pangs of death will not touch them. To the eyes of the foolish they seemed to die, but they are in peace," etc. This is the end of our wisdom, which, while it is sober and subject to God, at the same time knows, that those who aspire higher only procure a fall.

THE SLEEP OF THE SOUL

* * *

Let us now examine the cradle in which they rock souls asleep, and let us dispose of the soporiferous draught which they give them to drink. They carry about with them some passages of Scripture which seem to favor that sleep, and then, as if the fact of *sleeping* were clearly proved, fulminate against those who do not instantly subscribe to their error. They insist, *first*, that God did not infuse into man any other soul than that which is common to him with the brutes; for Scripture ascribes the same "living soul" to all alike; as where it is said, "God created the great whales and every living soul" (Gen. 2:21.). Again, "To each of all flesh in which was the breath of life" (Gen. 7:15), and other things to the same effect. And it is said, that even had the Sacred Writings elsewhere made no mention of the matter, we are distinctly reminded by the Apostle that that living soul differs in no respect from the present life with which the body vegetates, when he says,

> It is sown in corruption, it will rise in incorruption; it is sown in weakness, it will rise in power; it is sown an animal, it will rise a spiritual body; as it is written, The first Adam was made a living soul, the last Adam a quickening spirit (1 Cor. 15:42–45).

I admit that a *living soul* is repeatedly attributed to the brutes, because they, too, have their own life; but they live after one way, man after another. Man has a living soul by which he knows and understands; they have a living soul which gives their body sense and motion. Seeing, then, that the soul of man possesses reason, intellect, and will—qualities which are not annexed to the body—it is not wonderful that it subsists without the body, and does not perish like the brutes, which have nothing more than their bodily senses. Hence Paul was not ashamed to adopt the expression of a heathen poet, and call us the offspring of God (Acts 17:28). Let them, then, if they will, make a living soul common to man and to the brutes, since in so far as the body is concerned they have all the same life, but let them not employ this as an argument for confounding the soul of man with the brutes.

Nor let them obtrude upon me the Apostle's expression, which is more with me than against me. He says, "The first Adam was a living soul, the last Adam a quickening spirit" (1 Cor. 15:45).

His answer here corresponds to the question of those who could not be persuaded of the resurrection. They objected: How will the dead rise again? With what body will they come? The Apostle, to meet this objection, thus addresses them: If we learn by experience that the seed, which lives, grows, and yields fruit, has previously died, why may not the body after it has died rise again like a seed? And if dry and bare grain, after it has died, produces more abundant increase, by a wondrous virtue which God has implanted in it, why may not the body, by the same divine power, be raised better than it died? And that you may not wonder at this: How is it that man lives, but just because he was formed a living soul?

This soul, however, though for a time it actuates and sustains the bodily mass, does not impart to it immortality or incorruption, and as long even as it exerts its own energy; it is not sufficient by itself, without the auxiliaries of food, drink, sleep, which are the signs of corruption; nor does it maintain it in a constant and uniform state without being subject to various kinds of inclinations. But when Christ shall have received us into his own glory, not only will the animal body be quickened by the soul, but made spiritual in a manner which our mind can neither comprehend nor our tongue express (see Tertullian and August., Ep. 3, *ad Fortunat.*). You see, then, that in the resurrection we shall be not a *different thing*, but a *different person* (pardon the expression). These things have been said of the body, to which the soul ministers life under the elements of this world; but when the fashion of this world shall have passed away, participation in the glory of God will exalt it above nature.

We now have the genuine meaning of the Apostle's expression. Augustine, having once erred in expounding it, as those men now do, afterwards acknowledged his error, and inserted it among his *Retractations*. In another place he treats the whole subject with the greatest distinctness (*Retract.*, c. 10, Ep. 146, *Consentio*). I will make a few extracts:

> The soul indeed lives in an animal body, but does not quicken it so as to take away corruption; but when, in a spiritual body, adhering perfectly to the Lord, one spirit is formed, it so quickens it as to make it a spiritual body, consuming all corruption, fearing no separation.

In short, were I to grant them all they ask in regard to a living soul (on which expression, as I have already said, I do not found much), yet that seat of the image of God always remains safe, whether they call it "*soul*" or "*spirit*," or give it any other name.

It is not more difficult to refute their objection taken from Ezekiel 37:9, where the prophet, making a kind of supposititious resurrection, calls a spirit from the four winds to breathe upon the dry bones. From this they think themselves entitled to infer that the soul of man is nothing else than the power and faculty of motion without substance—a power and faculty which may become evanescent at death, and be again gathered together at the resurrection. As if I might not in the same way infer that the Spirit of God is either wind or evanescent motion, seeing that

Ezekiel himself, in his first vision, uses the term "*wind*" for the eternal Spirit of God! But to any man not altogether stupid it is easy to give the solution, though these good folks, from dullness or ignorance, observe it not. In both passages we see examples of what is occasionally occurring in the Prophets, who figure spiritual things too high for human sense by corporeal and visible symbols. Accordingly, when Ezekiel wished to give a distinct and, as it were, bodily representation of the Spirit of God and the spirit of man—a thing altogether impossible in regard to a spiritual nature—he borrowed a similitude from corporeal objects to serve as a kind of image.

Their *second* objection is that the soul, though endowed with immortality, lapsed into sin, and thereby sunk and destroyed its immortality. This was the appointed punishment for sin as denounced to our first parents: "Dying ye shall die" (Gen. 2:17). And Paul says, "The wages of sin is death" (Rom. 6:23). And the Prophet exclaims, that "The soul that sinneth shall die" (Ezek. 18:4). They quote other similar passages. But I ask, *first*, whether the same wages of sin were not paid to the Devil? And yet his death was not such as to prevent him from being always awake, going about seeking whom he may devour, and working in the children of disobedience. I ask, *secondly*, whether or not there is to be any end to that death? If none, as we must certainly acknowledge, then, although dead, they shall still feel eternal fire and the worm which does not die. These things make it manifest that the immortality of the soul, which we assert, and which we say consists in a perception of good and evil, exists even when it is dead, and that that death is something else than the annihilation to which they would reduce it.

Nor are the Scriptures silent on this point, could they bring their mind to submit their own views to Scripture, instead of arrogantly affirming whatever their dark and drowsy brains may dictate. When God pronounces this sentence against man as a sinner, "Dust thou art, and to dust shalt thou return," does he say more than that that which has been taken from the earth shall return to the earth? To where then does the soul go? Does it descend into the tomb, to rottenness and corruption? These points will be considered more fully soon. But now, why do they quibble? We have heard that that which is of the earth is to be returned to the earth. Why do we plunge the spirit of man under the earth? He says not that man will return to the earth, but that he who is dust will return to dust. But dust is that which was formed out of clay. It returns to dust, but not the spirit, which God derived from another quarter, and gave to man.

Accordingly, we read in the book of Job, "Remember how thou hast made me of clay, and will reduce me to dust" (Job 10:9). This is said of the body. A little after he adds, "Life and mercy hast thou given me, and thy visitation has preserved my spirit" (Job 10:12). That life, then, was not to return to dust.

* * *

The death of the soul is very different. It is the judgment of God, the weight of which the wretched soul cannot bear without being wholly confounded, crushed, and desperate, as both the Scriptures teach us, and experience has taught those whom God has once smitten with his terrors. To begin with Adam, who first received the fatal wages, what do we think his feelings must have been when he heard the dreadful question: "Adam, where are you?" It is easier to imagine than to express it, though imagination must fall far short of the reality. As the sublime majesty of God cannot be expressed in words, so neither can his dreadful anger on those on whom he inflicts it be expressed. They see the power of the Almighty actually present: to escape it, they would plunge themselves into a thousand abysses; but escape they cannot. Who does not confess that this is very death? Here I again say that they have no need of words who have at any time felt the stings of conscience; and let those who have not felt them only listen to the Scriptures, in which "our God" is described as "a consuming fire" (Exod. 20:19) and as slaying when he speaks in judgment. Such they knew him to be, who said, "Let not the Lord speak to us, lest we die!" (Deut. 18:16).

Would you know what the death of the soul is? It is to be without God—to be abandoned by God, and left to itself: for if God is its life, it loses its life when it loses the presence of

God. That which has been said in general may be shown in particular parts. If without God, there are no rays to illumine our night, surely the soul, buried in its own darkness, is *blind*. It is also *dumb*, not being able to confess unto salvation what it has believed unto righteousness. It is *deaf*, not hearing that living voice. It is *lame*, nay, unable to support itself, having none to whom it can say, "Thou hast held my right hand, and conducted me in thy will." In short, it performs no one function of life. For thus speaks the Prophet, when he would show that the fountain of life is with God:

> Learn where there is prudence, where there is virtue, where there is understanding, where there is length of life and food, where there is light to the eyes and peace (Bar. 3:14).

What more do you require for death? But, not to stop here, let us consider with ourselves what life Christ hath brought us, and then we shall understand what the death is from which he hath redeemed us. We are taught both by the Apostle, when he says, "Awake, thou that sleepest, and arise from the dead, and Christ will give thee light" (Eph. 5:14). Here it is not asses he addresses, but those who, entangled in sin, carry death and hell along with them. Again, "You, when you were dead in sins, hath he quickened together in Christ, forgiving you all trespasses" (Eph. 2:1).

Accordingly, as the Apostle says, that "we die to sin" (Col. 2:13) when concupiscence is extinguished in us, so we also die to God when we become subject to concupiscence living in us (Rom. 6:2). Nay (to comprehend in one word what he says of the widow living in pleasure), "while living we are dead" (1 Tim. 5:6); in other words, we are undying in regard to death. For although the mind retains its power of perception, yet evil concupiscence is, as it were, a kind of mental stupefaction.

Then, such death as the soul endures Christ underwent on our account; for all which the prophecies promised concerning his victory over death he performed by his death. The prophets declared, "He will overthrow death for ever" (Isa. 15:8). Again, "I will be thy death, O death! thy devourer, O hell!" (Hos. 13:14). The Apostles proclaim the accomplishment of these things, "He hath indeed destroyed death, and illumined life by the gospel" (Col. 2). And again, "If, by the fault of one, death reigned by one, much more shall those who have received exuberance of grace reign through life in Christ" (Rom. 5:17). Let them, if they can, resist these passages, which are not so much words as flashes of lightning!

When they say, what we indeed admit, that death is from Adam—death, however, not as they feign, but such as we have lately shown to be applicable to the soul—we, on the other hand, say that life is from Christ, and this they cannot deny. The whole controversy turns on a comparison between Adam and Christ. They must necessarily concede to the Apostle not only that everything which had fallen in Adam is renewed in Christ, but inasmuch as the power of grace was stronger than that of sin, so much has Christ been more powerful in restoring than Adam in destroying: for he distinctly declares that the gift is not as the sin, but is much more exuberant, not indeed by including a greater number of individuals, but by bestowing richer blessings on those whom it includes. Let them say, if they will, that it was exuberant, not by giving more abundant life, but by effacing many sins, seeing that the one sin of Adam had plunged us into ruin. I ask no more.

Again, when he elsewhere says, that "the sting of death was sin" (1 Cor. 15:56), how can death longer sting us, when its sting has been blunted, nay, destroyed? The whole scope of several chapters in the Epistle to the Romans is to make it manifest that sin is completely abolished so as no longer to have dominion over believers. Then, if the strength of sin is the law, what else do they, when they slay those who live in Christ, than subject them to the curse of the law from which they had been delivered? Hence the Apostle confidently declares that "there is now no condemnation to those who are in Christ Jesus, who walk not after the flesh, but after the Spirit" (Rom. 8:1). On those whom the Apostle thus frees from all condemnation, they pronounce the severest of all sentences, "Dying, ye shall die!" Where is grace, if death still reigns among the elect of God? Sin, as the Apostle says, indeed reigned unto death, but grace reigns unto eternal life, and, overcoming sin, leaves no place for death. Therefore, as death reigned on entering by Adam, so now life reigns by Jesus Christ. And we know that

> "Christ, being raised from the dead, dies no more: death shall no longer have dominion over him: For in that he died, he died unto sin once; but in that he lives, he lives unto God" (Rom. 6:9).

Here we may see how they themselves give their heresy its deathblow! When they say that "death is the punishment of sin," they at the same time imply that man, if he had not fallen, would have been immortal. What he began to be, he once was not; and what he is by punishment, he is not by nature. Then the Apostle exclaims that sin is absorbed by grace, so that it can no longer have any power over the elect of God; and hence we conclude that the elect now are such as Adam was before his sin; and as he was created inexterminable, so now have those become who have been renewed by Christ to a better nature. There is nothing at variance with this in the Apostle's declaration, "The word shall be accomplished [*fiet*], death has been swallowed up in victory" (1 Cor. 15:54), since no man can deny that the term *fiet* (shall be done) is synonymous with *implebitur* (shall be fulfilled). That shall be fulfilled in the body which has now been begun in the soul; or rather, that which has only been begun in the soul will be fulfilled both in the soul and the body: for this common death which we all undergo, as it were by a common necessity of nature, is rather to the elect a kind of passage to the highest degree of immortality, than either an evil or a punishment, and, as Augustine says is nothing else than the falling off of the flesh, which does not consume the things connected with it, but divides them, seeing it restores each to its original (*De Discrimine Vitae Human. et Brut.*, c. 43).

Their *third* argument is: That those who have died are in many places said to *sleep*, as in the case of Stephen: "He fell asleep in the Lord" (Acts 7:60); again, "Our Lazarus sleepeth" (John 11:11); again, "Be not anxious about them who are asleep" (1 Thess. 4:13). The same occurs so often in the books of Kings, that there is scarcely an expression which is more familiar. But the passage on which they most strenuously insist is taken from the book of Job:

> A tree has hope: if it is cut down it grows green again, and its branches bud forth, etc.; but when man has died and been laid bare and consumed, where is he? As when the waters of the sea recede, and the

channel left empty becomes dry, so man when he has fallen asleep will not rise nor be awakened out of his sleep till the heavens be crushed (Job 14:7–12).

But if you hold that souls sleep because death is called sleeping, then the soul of Christ must have been seized with the same sleep: for David thus speaks in his name, "I laid me down and slept; I rose up, for the Lord sustained me" (Psa. 3:6). And he hears his enemies in insult exclaiming, "Will he who sleeps rise again?" (Psa. 41:9). But if, as has been more fully discussed, nothing so mean and abject is to be imagined in regard to the soul of Christ, no man can doubt that the Scripture referred merely to the external composition of the body, and described it as sleep from so appearing to man. The two expressions are used indiscriminately: "he slept with his fathers;" "he was laid with his fathers"—although no man's soul is laid with the soul of his father's when his body is carried to their tomb. In the same sense, I think this sleep is attributed to impious kings, in the books of Kings and Chronicles.

When you hear that the wicked man *sleeps*, do you think of a sleep of his soul? It cannot have a worse executioner to torment it than an evil conscience. How can there be sleep amid such anguish? "The wicked are like the tempestuous sea which cannot rest, and whose waves cast up mire and dirt.

'There is no peace to the wicked,' saith the Lord" (Isa. 57:20-21).

And yet, when David wished to describe the bitterest pang of conscience, he says, "Enlighten my eyes, lest I sleep the sleep of death" (Psa. 13:4). The jaws of hell yawn to engulf him, the power of sin tosses him about, and yet he sleeps, nay, sleeps just because he so suffers! Here, too, we must send those back to their rudiments who have not yet learned that by synecdoche the whole is sometimes taken for a part, and sometimes a part for the whole—a figure which is constantly occurring in Scripture. I do not wish the fact to be taken on my word, but will produce passages to prove it.

When Job said, "Behold I now sleep in the dust, and if ye seek me in the morning I shall not subsist" (Job 7:21), did he think that his soul was to be overwhelmed with sleep? His soul was not to be thrown into the dust, and therefore was not to sleep in the dust. When he said in another passage, "And yet they shall sleep in the dust, and the worms shall cover them" (Job 21:26), and when David said, "Like the wounded sleeping in their tombs" (Psa. 88:6), do you think that they put souls down before worms to be gnawed by them?

To the same effect the Prophet, when describing the future destruction of Nebuchadnezzar says, "The whole land has rested and been silent, the fir-trees also and the cedars of Lebanon have rejoiced over thee; from the time at which thou didst fall asleep, no one has come up to hew us down" (Isa. 14:8.). A little after he says, "All the kings of the nations have slept in glory, each man in his place, but thou hast been cast forth from the tomb" (Isa. 14:18–19).

All these things were said of a dead body, "sleeping," being used as equivalent to lying or being stretched out, as sleepers do when stretched on the ground. This mode of expression might be taught us by profane writers, one of whom says, "When once our short light has set, an everlasting night must be slept;" and another, "Fool, what is sleep?" and again, "Let the bones of Naso lie softly." These expressions are used by writers who have many monstrous fictions respecting the lower regions, and describe the many and various feelings by which the shades of the dead are affected. Hence the very name given by the ancients to places destined for sepulture was κοιμητηριον (*koimētērion*, "cemetery," or "sleeping place"). They did not imagine that dead souls were then laid to rest, but spoke only of the body. I presume that I have now sufficiently disposed of the smoke in which they involved their "sleep of the soul" by proving that nowhere in Scripture is the term *sleep* applied to the soul, when it is used to designate death. We have elsewhere discoursed fully of "the rest of the soul."

The *fourth* argument which they urge against us, as their most powerful battering ram, is the passage in which Solomon thus writes in his Ecclesiastes,

I said in my heart of the children of men that God would prove them to show that they were like the brutes. As man dies, so do they also die. In like manner all things breathe, and man has no more than a beast of burden. All things are subject to vanity, and hasten to one place. Of earth have they been made, and to earth do they equally return. Who knows whether the spirit of the sons of Adam ascends upwards, and the spirit of beasts descends downwards? (3:18–21).

What if Solomon himself here answers them in one word? "Vanity of vanities, saith the Preacher, vanity of vanities, and all is vanity!" For what else does he aim at than to show the vain sense of man, and the uncertainty of all things? Man sees that he dies like the brutes, that he has life and death in common with them; and he therefore infers that his condition is on an equality with theirs: and as nothing remains to them after death, so he makes nothing remain to himself. This is the mind of man, this his reason, this his intellect! "For the animal man receiveth not the things of the Spirit; they are foolishness unto him, neither can he understand them" (1 Cor. 2:14).

Man looks with the eyes of flesh and beholds death present, and the only reflection he makes is, that all things have sprung from the earth, and equally return to the earth; meanwhile, he takes no account of the soul. And this is the meaning of the subjoined clause, "Who knows whether the spirit of the sons of Adam ascends upwards?" For if the subject of the soul is considered, human nature, wholly contracted in itself, comprehends nothing distinctly or clearly by studying, meditating, and reasoning.

Therefore, when Solomon shows the vanity of human sense, from the consideration, that in examining the mind, it fluctuates and is held in suspense, he by no means countenances their error, but nobly supports our faith. That which exceeds the capacity and little measure of the human mind, the wisdom of God explains, assuring us that the spirit of the sons of Adam ascends upwards. I will bring forward a similar passage from the same writer for the purpose of somewhat bending their stubborn neck.

> Man does not understand either the hatred or the love of God towards men, but all things are kept uncertain, because all things happen equally to the righteous and the wicked, the good and bad, to him sacrificing victims and to him not sacrificing (Eccl. 9:1).

If all things are kept uncertain in regard to the future, shall the believer, to whom all things work together for good, regard affliction as an evidence of divine hatred? By no means. For believers have been told, "In the world you shall have tribulation—in me, consolation." Supported by this consideration, they not only endure whatever befalls them with unshaken magnanimity, but even glory in tribulation, acknowledging with blessed Job, "Though he slay us, we will hope in him" (Job 13:15).

How, then, are all things kept uncertain in regard to the future? This is only humanly speaking. But every living man is vanity. He adds,

> The worst thing I have seen under the sun is, that the same things happen to all; hence the hearts of the children of men are filled with malice and contempt in their life, and afterwards are taken down to the lower regions. There is no man who can live always, or have expectation of such a thing. A living dog is better than a dead lion. For the living know that they shall die, but the dead no longer know anything. Nor have they further any Reward; for their memory is given up to oblivion, etc. (Eccl. 9:3–5).

Does he not speak thus of the gross stupidity of those who see only what is actually present, hoping neither for future life nor resurrection? For even if it were true that we are nothing after death, still the resurrection remains; and, would they fix their hopes on it, they would neither feel contempt for God, nor be filled with all kinds of wickedness, not to mention other things. Let us therefore conclude, with Solomon, that all these things are beyond the reach of human reason. But if we would have any certainty, let us run to the law and the testimony, where are the truth and the ways of the Lord. They declare to us, "Until the dust return to the earth whence it was, and the spirit return to God who gave it" (Eccl. 12:7).

Let no one, then, who has heard the word of the Lord, have any doubt that the spirit of the children of Adam ascends upwards. By "ascending upwards" in that passage, I understand simply subsisting and retaining immortality, just as "descending downwards" seems to me to mean lapsing, falling, becoming lost.

Their *fifth* argument they thunder forth with so much noise, that it might arouse the sleeping out of the deepest sleep. They place their greatest hope of victory in it, and, when they would gloss over matters to their neophytes, place most dependence upon it as a means of shaking their faith and overcoming their good sense. There is one judgment, they say, which will render to all their reward—to the pious, glory; to the impious, hell fire. No blessedness or misery is fixed before that day. This the Scriptures uniformly declare, "He will send his angels with a trumpet and a loud voice, and they will assemble his elect from the four winds, from the heights of heaven to the utmost limits thereof" (Matt 24:31).

Again,

> At the end of the world, the Son of man will send his angels, and they will gather out of his kingdom all things that offend, and those who do iniquity, and will send them into the furnace of fire. Then the righteous will shine forth like the sun in the kingdom of their Father (Matt. 13:41–43).

Again,

> Then will the King say to them on his right hand, Come, ye blessed of my Father, inherit the kingdom prepared for you from the foundation of the world. . . . Depart from me, ye cursed, into everlasting fire. . . . And they shall go away, the latter to eternal punishment, and the former to eternal life (Matt. 25:34–41).

To the same effect is the passage in Daniel 12, "And in that time shall thy people be saved, all of them whose names shall be found written in the book."

They ask: If all these things have been written of the Day of Judgment, how will the elect be then called to the possession of the heavenly kingdom, if they already possess it? How can they be told to come, if they are already there? How will the people be then saved if they are safe now? Wherefore believers, who even now walk in faith, do not expect any other day of salvation, as Paul says, "Knowing that he who raised up Jesus from the dead will also raise us up with Jesus" (2 Cor. 4:14). And elsewhere, "Waiting for the revelation of our Lord Jesus Christ, who will confirm us even unto the end, against the day of his approach," etc.

But though we were to concede all these things to them, why do they make their own addition about "sleep?" For in all these, and similar passages, they cannot produce one syllable concerning sleep. Though they be awake, they may be without glory. Wherefore, since it is the part of a senseless, not to say presumptuous man, to decide peremptorily, without any authority from Scripture, on points which do not fall under human sense, with what countenance do those new and swollen dogmatists proceed to maintain a sleep of which they have heard nothing from the lips of our Lord? All persons of sense and soberness may hence see that a sleep which cannot be proved from the plain word of God is a wicked fiction. But let us take up the passages in order, lest the more simple be moved when they hear that the salvation of souls is deferred to the day of judgment.

First, we wish it to be held as an acknowledged point, as we have already explained, that our blessedness is always in progress up to that day which shall conclude and terminate all progress, and that thus the glory of the elect, and complete consummation of hope, look forward to that day for their fulfillment. For it is admitted by all, that perfection of blessedness or glory nowhere exists except in perfect union with God. Hither we all tend, hither we hasten, hither all the Scriptures and the divine promises send us. For that which was once said to Abraham applies to us also: "Abraham, I am thy exceeding great reward" (Gen. 15:1). Seeing, then, that the reward appointed for all who have part with Abraham is to possess God and enjoy him, and that, besides and beyond it, it is not lawful to long for any other, thither must our eyes be turned when the subject of our expectation is considered. Thus far, if I mistake not, our opponents are agreed with us.

On the other hand, I hope they will concede that that kingdom, to the possession of which we are called, and which is elsewhere denominated "salvation," and "reward," and "glory," is nothing else than that union with God by which they are fully in God, are filled by God, in their turn cleave to God, completely possess God—in short, are "one with God." For thus, while they are in the fountain of all fullness, they reach the ultimate goal of righteousness, wisdom, and glory, these being the blessings in which the kingdom of glory consists. For Paul intimates that the kingdom of God is in its highest perfection when "God is all in all" (1 Cor. 15:28). Since on that day, only God will be all in all, and completely fill his believers, it is called, not without reason, "the day of our salvation," before which our salvation is not perfected in all its parts. For those whom God fills are filled with riches which neither ear can hear, nor eye see, nor tongue tell, nor imagination conceive.

If these two points are beyond controversy, our hypnologists (sleep maintainers) in vain endeavor to prove that the holy servants of God, on departing this life, do not yet enter the kingdom of God, from its being said, "Come"; "inherit the kingdom"; and so forth. For it is easy for us to answer that it does not follow that there is no kingdom because there is not a perfect one; on the contrary, we maintain that that which has been already begun is then to be perfected. This I only wish to be conceded to me when I shall have made it plain by sure Scripture argument.

That day is called "the kingdom of God," because he will then make adverse powers truly subject, slay Satan by the breath of his mouth, and destroy him by the brightness of his coming, while he himself will wholly dwell and reign in his elect (1 Cor. 15:24; 2 Thess. 2:8). God in himself cannot reign otherwise than he reigned from the beginning. Of his majesty there cannot be increase or diminution. But it is called "His kingdom," because it will be manifested to all. When we pray that his kingdom may come, do we imagine that previously it exists not? And when will it be? "The kingdom of God is within you" (Luke 17:21). God, therefore, now reigns in his elect whom he guides by his Spirit. He reigns also in opposition to the devil, sin, and death, when he bids the light, by which error and falsehood are confounded, to shine out of darkness and when he prohibits the powers of darkness from hurting those who have the mark of the Lamb in their foreheads. He reigns, I say, even now, when we pray that his kingdom may come. He reigns, indeed, while he performs miracles in his servants, and gives the law to Satan. But his kingdom will properly come when it will be completed. And it will be completed when he will plainly manifest the glory of his majesty to his elect for salvation, and to the reprobate for confusion.

And what else is to be said or believed of the elect, whose kingdom and glory it is to be in the glorious kingdom of God, and as it were reign with God and glory in him—in short, to be partakers of the Divine glory? This kingdom, though it is said not yet to have come, may yet be in some measure beheld. For those who in a manner have the kingdom of God within them, and reign with God, begin to be in the kingdom of God; the gates of hell cannot prevail against them. They are justified in God, it being said of them, "In the Lord will all the seed of Israel be justified and praised" (Isa. 45:25).

That kingdom wholly consists in the building up of the Church, or the progress of believers, who, as described to us by Paul, grow up through all the different stages of life into "a perfect man" (Eph. 4:13).

These good folks see the beginnings of this kingdom—see the increase. As soon as these disappear from their eyes, they give no place to faith, and are unable to believe what the eye of flesh has ceased to behold. Very different is the conduct of the Apostle! He says, "Ye are dead, and your life is hid with Christ in God. When Christ your life shall appear, then shall ye also appear with him in glory" (Col. 3:4).

He indeed attributes to us a hidden life with Christ our Head beside God; he delays the glory to the day of the glory of Christ, who, as the Head of the Church, will bring his members with him. The very same thing is expressed by John, though in different terms:

> Beloved, now are we the sons of God; but it hath not yet appeared what we shall be: but we know that when he shall appear, we shall be like him, since we shall see him as he is (1 John 3:2).

He says not that meanwhile, for some length of time, we shall be nothing; but, seeing we are the sons of God, who wait for the inheritance of the Father, he keeps up and suspends our expectation, till that day on which the glory of Christ will be manifest in all, and we shall be glorified in him. Here, again, we cannot help wondering that, when they hear of "sons of God," they do not return to a sound mind, and perceive that this is an immortal generation which is of God, and by which we are partakers of a Divine immortality. But to proceed.

Let them cry out, as much as they please, that they are not called the blessed of God before the day of judgment, and that not before it is salvation promised to the people of God.

I answer, that Christ is our Head, whose kingdom and glory have not yet appeared: if the members precede, the order is perverted and preposterous. We shall follow our Prince when he shall come in the glory of his Father, and sit in the seat of his majesty. Meanwhile, there is life in all within us that is of God—that is, our spirit, because Christ our life lives. For it were absurd to say we perish, while our life is living! This life is both beside God and with God, and is blessed because it is in God.

All these things are self-evident, and in accordance with the truth. Why are those who have died in the Lord said to be not yet saved, or not yet to possess the kingdom of God? Because they wait for what they as yet have not, and have not reached the summit of their felicity. Why are they, nevertheless, happy? Because they both perceive God to be propitious to them, and see their future reward from a distance, and rest in the sure hope of a blessed resurrection. As long as we dwell in this prison of clay, we hope for what we see not, and against hope believe in hope, as the Apostle says of Abraham (Rom. 4:18). But when the eyes of our mind, now dull because buried in flesh, shall have thrown off this dullness, we shall see what we waited for, and be delighted in that rest. We are not afraid to speak thus, after the Apostle, who says conversely, that a fearful looking for of judgment awaits the reprobate (Heb. 10:27). If this is called "fearful," the other surely may be justly called "joyful" and "blessed."

Since it is more my purpose to instruct than to crush my opponents, let them lend me their ear for a little, while we extract the reality from a figure of the Old Testament, and that not without authority. As Paul, in speaking of the passage of the Israelites across the Red Sea, allegorically represents the drowning of Pharaoh as the mode of deliverance by water (1 Cor. 10:1), so we may be permitted to say that in baptism our Pharaoh is drowned, our old man is crucified, our members are mortified, we are buried with Christ, and remove from the captivity of the devil and the power of death, but remove only into the desert, a land arid and poor, unless the Lord rain manna from heaven, and cause water to gush forth from the rock.

For our soul, like that land without water, is in want of all things, till he, by the grace of his Spirit, rain upon it. We afterwards pass into the land of promise, under the guidance of Joshua the son of Nun, into a land flowing with milk and honey; that is, the grace of God frees us from the body of death, by our Lord Jesus Christ, not without sweat and blood, since the flesh is then most repugnant, and exerts its utmost force in warring against the Spirit. After we take up our residence in the land, we feed abundantly. White robes and rest are given us. But Jerusalem, the capital and seat of the kingdom, has not yet been erected; nor yet does Solomon, the Prince of Peace, hold the scepter and rule over all.

The souls of the saints, therefore, which have escaped the hands of the enemy, are after death in peace. They are amply supplied with all things, for it is said of them, "They shall go from abundance to abundance." But when the heavenly Jerusalem shall have risen up in its glory, and Christ, the true Solomon, the Prince of Peace, shall be seated aloft on his tribunal, the true Israelites will reign with their King. Or—if you choose to borrow a similitude from the affairs of men—we are fighting with the enemy, so long as we have our contest with flesh and blood; we conquer the enemy when we put off the body of sin, and become wholly God's; we will celebrate our triumph, and enjoy the fruits of victory, when our head shall be raised above death in glow, that is, when death shall be swallowed up in victory. This is our aim, this our goal; and of this it has been written, "I shall be satisfied when I awake with beholding thy glory" (Psa. 17:15). These things may be easily learned Scripture, by all who have learned to hear God and hearken to his voice.

The same things have been handed down to us by tradition, from those who have cautiously and reverently handled the mysteries of God. For ancient writers, while declaring that souls are indeed in paradise, and in heaven, have not hesitated to say that they have not yet received their glory and reward. Tertullian says, "Both the reward and the peril depend on the event of the Resurrection" (Lib. *de Resurrect. Carnis*). And yet he teaches, without any ambiguity, that "previously to that event souls are with God, and live in God." In another place he says,

> Why do we not comprehend that by Abraham's bosom is meant a temporary receptacle of faithful souls, wherein the image of faith is delineated, and a clear view of both judgments exhibited?

The words of Irenaeus are,

> Since our Lord departed, in the midst of the shadow of death, to the place where the souls of the dead were, thereafter rose again bodily, and after his Resurrection was taken up, it is manifest, both that the souls of his disciples, on whose account the Lord performed these things, will go away into the invisible place assigned them by the Lord, and there remain until the Resurrection, waiting for the Resurrection; afterwards recovering their bodies, and rising again perfectly, that is, bodily, as the Lord also rose, they will come into the presence of God. "For the disciple is not above his Master," etc. (Lib. 9, *adv. Haeres*).

Chrysostom says,

> Understand what and how great a thing it is for Abraham to sit and the Apostle Paul, when he is perfected, that they may then be able to receive their reward. Unless we come thither the Father hath foretold us that he will not give the reward, as a good father who loves his children says to probable children and those finishing their labor, that he will not give food till the other brothers have come. Are you anxious because you do not yet receive? What then will Abel do, who formerly conquered, and still sits without a crown? What will Noah do? What the others of those times? Lo! they have waited and still wait for others who are to be after thee.... They were before us in the contest, but they will not be before us in the crown; for there is one set time for all the crowns (Hom. 28, in 11 *ad Hebr.*).

Augustine, in many passages, describes the secret receptacles in which the souls of the righteous are kept until they receive the crown and the glory, while meanwhile the reprobate suffer punishment, waiting for the precise measure to be fixed by the judgment (*De Civitate*, Lib. 12 c. 9; Lib. 13 c. 8, et. alibi). And in an Epistle to Jerome he says, "The soul after the death of the body will have rest, and will at length receive the body into glory." Bernard, professedly handling this question in two sermons delivered on the Feast of All Saints, teaches, that "the souls of the saints, divested of their bodies, still stand in the courts of the Lord, admitted to rest but not yet to glory. Into that most blessed abode," he says, "they shall neither enter without us, nor without their own bodies;" that is, neither saints without other believers, nor spirits without flesh: and many other things to the same purpose.

Those who place them in heaven, provided they do not attribute to them the glory of the Resurrection, do not differ from that view. This Augustine himself, in another place, apparently does (*de Ecclesiastes Dogmat.*). For while it is certain that wicked demons are now tormented (as Peter affirms in chapter 2), yet that fire into which the reprobate will be sent on the Day of Judgment, is said here to be prepared for the devil (Jude). Both things are expressed when it is said, that they are "reserved in eternal chains against the judgment of the great day;"—"reserved" here intimating the punishment which they as yet feel not, and "chains" the punishment which they actually endure. And Augustine explains himself in another passage, in Psalm 36, where he says,

> Assuredly your last day cannot be far distant. Prepare yourself for it. Such as you depart this life, such will you be restored to that life. After that life you shall not instantly be where the saints will be, to whom it will be said, "Come, ye blessed of my

Father, inherit the kingdom which was prepared for you from the foundation of the world." That you shall not yet be there every one knows; but you shall be where the proud and niggardly rich man in the midst of his torments saw the poor beggar, who was formerly covered with sores, resting far away. Placed in that rest you will wait secure against the day of judgment, when you will recover your body, when you will be changed and made like the angels.

Nor do I object to the illustration which he elsewhere gives, provided a sound and moderate interpretation be given to it, namely, that

> there are many states of soul, *first,* animation; *second,* sense; *third,* art; *fourth,* virtue; *fifth,* tranquillity; *sixth,* ingress; *seventh,* contemplation: or, if you rather choose it, *first,* of the body; *second,* to the body; *third,* about the body; *fourth,* to itself; *fifth,* in itself; *sixth,* to God; *seventh,* with God" (*de Quantitat. Animae*).

I have been induced to quote these words of the holy writer, rather to show what his views were, than with the idea of binding any one, or even myself, to adopt these distinctions. Even Augustine himself, I think, did not wish this, but was desirous, though in the plainest manner possible, to explain the progress of the soul: showing how it does not reach its final perfection until the Day of Judgment. It, moreover, occurred to me, that those who so much insist on this Day of Judgment may by means of it be convinced of their error. For in the Creed, which is the compendium of our faith, we confess the resurrection, not of the soul, but of the body. There is no room for the cavil, that by "body" is meant the whole man. We admit; that it sometimes has this signification, but we cannot admit it here, where significant and simple expressions are used, in accommodation to the illiterate. Certainly the Pharisees, strong asserters of the resurrection, and constantly having the term in their mouths, at the same time believed it was not spirit.

Still, however, they insist, and keep us to the point, quoting the words in which Paul declares that "we are of all men the most miserable" if the dead rise not (1 Cor. 15:19).

What need is there of the resurrection, they ask, if we are happy before the resurrection? Nay, where is the great misery of Christians, a misery surpassing that which all others suffer, if it is true that they are in rest while others are afflicted and strongly tortured? Here I must tell them that if I had any desire to evade the difficulty (a thing on which they are always intent), I have here ample opportunity. For what hinders us from adopting the view taken by some sensible expositors, who understand the words to be spoken not only of the final resurrection, by which we shall recover our bodies from corruption, incorruptible; but of the life which remains to us after our mortal life is over, and which is frequently designated in Scripture by the name of resurrection? For when it is said that the Sadducees deny the resurrection, it is not the body that is referred to, but the simple meaning is, that, according to their opinion, nothing of man survives death.

This view is made probable by the fact, that all the grounds on which the Apostle founds his statement might have been obviated by answering that the soul indeed lives, but that the body, when once it has moldered into dust, cannot possibly be raised. Let us furnish specimens. When he says, "Those who have fallen asleep in Christ have perished," he might have been refuted by the philosophers who strenuously asserted the immortality of the soul. When he asks, "What will those do who are baptized for the dead?" he might easily have been answered that souls survive death. To the question, "Why are we in jeopardy every hour?" The reply might have been that we expose this frail life for the immortality in which our better part will live.

* * *

We have now said much for which there would have been no occasion among persons of teachable disposition. For the Apostle himself says, that we are miserable if we have hope in Christ in this life only. This is clear beyond dispute, even he being witness, who acknowledges that his feet were almost gone, and that this steps had well-nigh slipped when he saw sinners enjoying themselves on the earth. And certainly, if we look only to the present, we will call those happy to whom everything turns out to a wish. But if we extend our views farther, we see that happy is the people whose God is the Lord, for in his hands are the issues of death.

We can adduce something still more decided, not only to refute their objections, but to explain the genuine meaning of the Apostle to these who are willing to learn without being disputatious. For if there is no resurrection of the flesh, he justly for this one reason calls the pious unhappy, because they endure so many wounds, scourges, torments, contumely, in short, necessities of all kinds in their bodies, which they think destined to immortality; seeing they will be disappointed in this their expectation. For what can be, I do not say "more miserable," but even more ridiculous, than to see the bodies of those who live for the day indulging in all kinds of delicacies, while the bodies of Christians are worn out with hunger, cold, stripes, and all kinds of contumely, if the bodies of both equally perish! I might compare this by the words which follow: "Why are we in jeopardy every hour, I die daily through your glory, brethren," etc. "Let us eat and drink, for tomorrow we die." It were better, he says, to act on the maxim, "Let us eat," etc., if the affronts which we suffer in our bodies are not compensated by that glory for which we hope! This cannot be unless by the resurrection of the flesh. Then, though this were given up, I can adduce another argument, namely, we are more miserable than all men if there is no resurrection, because, although we are happy *before* the resurrection, we are not happy *without* the resurrection. For we say that the spirits of saints are happy in this, that they rest in the hope of a blessed resurrection, which they could not do, were all this blessedness to perish. True, there is the declaration of Paul, that we are more miserable than all men if there is no resurrection; and there is no repugnance in these words to the dogma, that the spirits of the just are blessed before the resurrection, since it is because of the resurrection.

They also bring forward what is said in the Epistle to the Hebrews concerning the ancient Patriarchs:

> All these died in faith, not having received the promises, but seeing them afar off, because they were strangers and pilgrims on the earth. For them who say so show that they seek a country. And, indeed, had they remembered the country from which they came, they had opportunity of returning, but now they desire a better, that is, a heavenly country (Heb. 11:13–16).

Here our opponents argue as follows: If they desire a heavenly country, they do not already possess it. We, on the contrary, argue: If they desire, they must exist, for there cannot be desire without a subject in which it resides. And, as I attempt to force from them only, there must be a sense of good and evil where there is desire which either follows what carries an appearance of good, or shows that which appears evil. That desire, they say, lies in God, than which nothing can be imagined more ridiculous. For one of two things must follow—either that God desires something better than he has, or that there is something in God which belongs not to God. This circumstance makes me suppose that they are merely sporting with a serious matter.

To omit this, what is meant by "the power of returning?" Let them, then, return to a sound mind and listen to something better than they have yet embraced; if, indeed, they are really persuaded of that which they profess with their lips. The Apostle is speaking of Abraham and his posterity who dwelt in a foreign land among strangers; only not exiles, but certainly sojourners, scarcely sheltering their bodies by living in poor huts, in obedience to the command of God given to Abraham, that he should leave his land and his kindred. God had promised them what he had not yet exhibited. Therefore they trusted the promises afar off, and died in the firm belief that the promises of God would one day be fulfilled. In accordance with this belief, they confessed that they had no fixed abode on the earth, and that beyond the earth there was a country for which they longed, namely, heaven. In the end of the chapter he intimates that all those whom he enumerated did not obtain the final promise that they might not be perfected without us. Had they attended to the peculiar meaning of this expression, they never would have excited so much disturbance. It is strange how they can be blind in so much light; but still more strange that they give us bread instead of stones—in other words, support our views while seeking to overthrow them!

They think they derive strong support from what is said in the Acts of the Apostles concerning Tabitha, who, when a disciple of Christ, full of alms and good deeds, was raised from the dead by Peter (Acts 9:40). They say, an injury was done to Tabitha, if we are correct in holding that the soul, when freed from the body, lives with God and in God, since she was brought back from the society of God and a life of blessedness to this evil world. As if the same thing might not be retorted upon them! For whether she slept, or was nothing, yet as she had died in the Lord she was blessed. It was, therefore, not expedient for her to return to the life which she had finished. They must themselves, therefore, first untie the knot which they have made, since it is but fair that they obey the law which they lay upon others. And yet it is easy for us to untie it.

Whatever be the lot which awaits us after death, what Paul says of himself, is applicable to all believers: "for us to die is gain, and to be with Christ is better" (Phil. 1:23). And yet Paul says that Epaphroditus, who certainly was in the number of believers, "obtained mercy of the Lord when sick nigh unto death," he recovered (Phil. 2:27). Those men, indeed, who handle the mysteries of God with so little reverence and sobriety, would interpret that mercy as cruelty. We, however, feel and acknowledge it to be mercy, seeing it is a step of Divine mercy to sanctify the elect and glorify the sanctified. Does not the Lord then display his mercy when he sanctifies us more and more? What! If the will of God is to be magnified in our body by life, as Paul says, is it not mercy? It is not surely ours to lay down laws for the miraculous works of God; it is enough if the glory of their author shine forth in them. What if we should say that God did not consult the advantage of Tabitha, but had respect to the poor at whose prayers she was raised up, while they kept weeping and showing the garments which Tabitha was wont to sew for them? Paul thought that this mode of living sufficed him, though it were far better for him to depart to God.

After saying that God had had mercy on Epaphroditus, he adds, "And not on him only, but on me also, that I might not have sorrow upon sorrow." Go now and raise a plea against God for having given back to the poor a woman who was diligent in supplying their wants! For, however the operation may appear to us, Christ, who died and rose again, that he might rule over the living and the dead, is certainly entitled to be glorified both in our life and in our death.

David also, the best defender of our cause, they call in as a defender of theirs, but with so much effrontery, and in a manner so devoid of common sense, that one is both ashamed and pained to mention the arguments which they borrow from him. The whole, however, with which we are acquainted we shall now honestly state.

First, they venture to quote the words: "I said, Ye are gods, and all of you exalted sons, but ye shall die like men," etc. (Psa. 82:6). And they interpret that believers are indeed gods and sons of God, but that they die and fall with the reprobate so that there is the same lot to both till the lambs shall be separated from the kids. We give the answer which we have received from Christ that "they are there called gods to whom the word of God came" (John 10:34); that is, ministers of God, namely, judges who bear in their hands the sword which they have received from God. Even had we not the interpretation of Christ and the usage of Scripture, which everywhere concurs, there is no obscurity in the passage itself, in which those are rebuked who judge iniquity and respect the faces of sinners. They are called gods, because acting as the representatives of God while they preside over others; but they are reminded of a future Judge to whom they must give an account of their office. See a specimen of the way in which our opponents argue!

Let us attend to another. It is said, *secondly* in Psalm 146:4, "His spirit will go forth and return to its earth. In that day all their thoughts perish." Here they take "spirit" for *wind* and say that the man will go away into the earth; that there will be nothing but earth; that all his thoughts will perish; whereas if there were any life they would remain. We are not so subtle, but in our dull way call a boat, a boat, and spirit, spirit! When this spirit departs from man, the man returns to the ground out of which he was taken, as we have fully explained. It remains, therefore, to see what is meant by thoughts "perishing." We are admonished not to put trust in men. Trust ought to be immortal. It were otherwise uncertain and unstable, seeing that the life of man passes quickly away. To intimate this, he said, that "their thoughts perish;" that is, that whatever they designed while alive is dissipated and given to the winds. Elsewhere he says, "The sinner will see and be angry; he will gnash with his teeth and pine away; the desire of the sinner will perish" (Psa. 112:10), as it is said in another place, "dissipated:" "The Lord dissipates the counsels of the heathen:" again, "Form a scheme and it will be dissipated" (Isa. 8:10). The same thing, in the form of a circumlocution, is expressed by the blessed Virgin in her song, "He hath dispersed the proud in the imagination of their hearts" (Luke 1:51).

A *third* passage which they adduce is taken from the Psalms: "And he remembered that they are flesh, the spirit going and not returning" (Psa. 78:39). They here contend, as they uniformly do, that "spirit" is used for wind. In this they perceive not that they not only destroy the immortality of the soul, but also cut off all hope of resurrection. For if there is a resurrection, the spirit certainly returns; and if it does not return, there is no resurrection! Wherefore, they ought here rather to implore pardon for their imprudence than insist on such a concession being made to them. Thus much I have said merely to let all men see how easily I might be quit were it my only object to refute their arguments. For we willingly admit, in accordance with their assertion, that the term *wind* is here applicable. We grant that men are "a wind which flies and returns not:" but if they wrest this to their own views, they err, not knowing the Scriptures, with which it is common by that kind of circumlocution to intimate at one time the weakness of man's condition, at another the shortness of life.

When Job says of man: "He is a flower which cometh forth, and is cut down, and fleeth as a shadow" (14:1), what more did he mean than just to say that man is fleeting, and frail, and like a fading flower? Isaiah again is ordered to exclaim,

> All flesh is grass, and all the glory of man as the flower of the grass; the grass withereth, and the flower thereof hath fallen away; but the word of the Lord endureth for ever (40:6).

Here let them infer, in one word, that the soul of man withers and pines away, and see a little more acutely than the dull fisherman who proves from it that all believers are immortal, because born again of incorruptible seed—that is, the word of God, which endureth for ever. Scripture gives the name of "fading flower" and "passing wind" to those who put their trust in this life. Having here as it were fixed their permanent abode, they think they are to reign without end; not looking to the end by which their condition is to be changed, and they must go elsewhere. Of such persons the Prophet also says, "We have stipulated with death, and made a compact with hell" (Isa. 28:15). Deriding their vain hope, he does not account as life that which is to them the beginning of the worst death. And he affirms that they cease and die, since it were better for them not to be than be what they are.

To the same effect we read in another Psalm,

> As a father pitieth his children, so the Lord pitieth all that fear him. For he knoweth our frame, he remembereth that we are dust. And man is as grass, his day is a flower of the field, so will he flourish. For his spirit will pass away in him, and he will not subsist, and he shall no longer know his place (103:13–16).

If they affirm from these verses that the spirit perishes and vanishes away, I again warn them not to open a door for atheists, if there are any such, to rise up and endeavor to overthrow their faith and ours in the resurrection, as there are certainly many. For in the same way they will infer that the spirit does not return to the body, seeing it is said that it shall no longer know its place. They may say, the inference is erroneous, since such arguing is plainly in the face of the passages relating to the resurrection; but I rejoice that their inference also is erroneous, since the mode of arguing is common to both.

Almost similar to this is the passage in Ecclesiasticus,

> The number of the years of man, as much as a hundred years, have been counted as the drop of water in the sea, and as the sand on the sea shore; but they are few compared with the whole duration of time. Therefore God is patient towards them, and sheds out his mercy upon them (18:8–10).

Here they must admit that the prophet's sentiment was very different; from that which they dream, and means that the Lord pitied those whom he knew to stand by his mercy alone, and, who, were he for a little to withdraw his hand, would return to the dust whence they were taken. Thereafter he subjoins a brief description of human life, comparing it to a flower which, though it blooms today, will be nothing more than dead herbage tomorrow.

Had he even declared that the spirit of man perishes and comes to nothing, he would not have given any defense to their error. For when we say that the spirit of man is immortal, we do not affirm that it can stand against the hand of God, or subsist without his agency. Far from us be such blasphemy! But we say that it is sustained by his hand and blessing. Thus Irenaeus, who with us asserts the immortality of the spirit (*adv. Haeres.* lib. 5), wishes us, however, to learn that by nature we are mortal, and God alone immortal. And in the same place he says,

> Let us not be inflated and raise ourselves up against God, as if we had life of ourselves; and let us learn by experience that we have endurance for eternity through his goodness, and not from our nature.

Our whole controversy with David then, whom they insist on making our opponent, is simply this: He says in Psalm 39:11 that man, if the Lord withdraw his mercy from him, falls away and perishes; we teach, that he is supported by the kindness and power of God, since he alone has immortality, and that whatever life exists is from him.

A *fourth* passage which they produce is,

> My soul is filled with evil, and my life has drawn near to hell. I am counted with those who go down into the deep, like a man without a helper, like the slain sleeping in their tombs, of whom thou art no longer mindful, they having been cut off from thy hand (Psa. 88:4).

What! They ask, if they have been cut off from the energy of God, if they have fallen away from his care and remembrance, have they not ceased to be? As if I had it not in my power to retort. What! If they have been cut off from the energy of God, if they have escaped his remembrance, how will they ever again be? And when will the Resurrection be? Again, how do the things agree? "The souls of the just are in the hands of God" (Wisd. 3:1); or, to quote only from the sure oracles of God, "The just will be in eternal remembrance" (Psa. 112:6).

They have not therefore fallen from the hand of the Lord, nor escaped his remembrance. Nay, rather, in this mode of expression, let us perceive the deep feelings of an afflicted man, who complains before God that he is almost abandoned with the wicked to perdition, whom God is said not to know and to have forgotten; because their names are not written in the book of life; and to have been cut away from his hand:, because he does not guide them by his Spirit.

The *fifth* passage is,

> Wilt thou do wonders to the dead, or will physicians raise them up, and they will confess to thee? Will any one narrate thy mercy in the tomb, or thy righteousness in the land of forgetfulness? (Psa. 88:11).

Again, "The dead will not praise thee, O Lord, nor all who descend into the lower parts; but we who live bless the Lord from this time, yea, even for ever" (Psa. 115:17).

Again, "What utility is there in my blood when I shall have descended into corruption? Will the dust confess to thee, or announce thy truth?" (Psa. 30:9).

To these passages they join another of very similar import from the song of Hezekiah,

> For the grave will not confess to thee, nor will death praise thee: those who descend into the pit will not wait for thy truth. The living, the living he will confess, to thee, as I too do today; the father will make known thy truth to his children (Isa 38:18–20).

They add from Ecclesiasticus, "From the dead, as being nothing, there is nothing; there is no confession. Thou the living wilt confess" (17:26).

We answer, that in these passages the term "dead" is not applied simply to those who have paid the common debt of nature when they depart this life: nor is it simply said that the praises of God cease at death; but the meaning partly is, that none will sing praises to the Lord save those who have felt his goodness and mercy; and partly, that his name is not celebrated after death, because his benefits are not, there declared among men as on the earth. Let us consider all the passages, and handle them in order, so that we may give to each its proper meaning.

First, let us learn this much, that though by death the dissolution of the present life is repeatedly signified, and by the lower region (*infernus*), the grave, yet it is no uncommon thing for Scripture to employ these terms for the anger and withdrawal of the power of God; so that persons are said to die and descend into the lower region, or to dwell in the lower region, when they are alienated from God, or prostrated by the judgment of God, or crushed by his hand. The lower region itself (*infernus ipse*) may signify, not the grave, but abyss and confusion. And this meaning, which occurs throughout Scripture, is most familiar in the Psalms: "Let death come upon them, and let them go down alive into the pit" (*infernum*) (Psa. 55:15). Again, "O my God, be not silent, lest I become like those who go down into the pit" (*lacum*) (Psa. 28:1). Again, "O Lord, thou hast brought up my soul from the lower region (*inferno*) and saved me from these going down into the pit" (*lacum*) (Psa. 30:3–4). Again, "Let sinners be turned into *infernus*, and all the nations which forget God" (Psa. 9:18). Again, "Had not the Lord assisted me, my soul had almost dwelt in *infernus*" (Psa. 94:17). Again, "Our bones have been scattered along *infernus*" (Psa. 141:7). Again, "He hath placed me in dark places, like the dead of the world" (Psa. 143:3).

In the New Testament, where the Evangelists use the term ᾅδης (*hadēs*), the translator has rendered it by *infernus*. Thus, it is said of the rich man, "When he was in hell" (*infernus*), etc. (Luke 16:23.) Again, "And thou, Capernaum, shalt thou be exalted unto heaven? Verily I say unto thee, thou shalt descend even unto hell" (*infernus*) (Matt. 11:23). In these places it signifies not so much the locality, as the condition of those whom God has condemned and doomed to destruction. And this is the confession which we make in the Creed, that Christ "descended into hell" (*in inferos*); in other words, that he was subjected by the Father, on our account, to all the pains of death; that he endured all its agonies and terrors, and was truly afflicted, it having been previously said that "he was buried."

On the other hand, those are said to *live*, and be about to live, whom the Lord visits in kindness: "For there the Lord hath commanded the blessing and life even for evermore" (Psa. 133:3). Again, "That he may deliver their souls from death, and nourish them in famine" (Psa. 33:19). Again, "The Lord will pluck thee up from thy tabernacle, and thy root from the land of the living" (Psa. 52:7). Again, "I will please the Lord in the region of the living" (Psa. 56:14).

To make a conclusion, let one passage suffice us, which so graphically depicts both conditions as fully to explain its own meaning, without our saying a word: It is in Psalm 49,

> Those who confide in much strength and glory in the multitude of riches. The brother does not redeem, will man redeem? Will he not give his own atonement to God, and the price of redemption for his soul, and labor for ever, and still live even to the end? Shall he not see death, when he shall see the wise dying? The unwise and the foolish will perish together. Like sheep they have been laid in the grave (*infernus*). Death shall feed upon them; and the just will rule over them in the morning, and assistance will perish in the grave (infernus), from their glory. Nevertheless God will redeem my soul from the hand of hell (*infernus*), when He will receive me.

The sum is, those who trust in their riches and strength will die and descend into *infernus*; the rich and the poor, the foolish and the wise, will perish together: he who hopes in the Lord will be free from the power of hell, (*infernus.*)

I maintain that these names—*death* and *hell* (*mors et infernus*)—cannot have any other meaning in the verses of the Psalms which they obtrude upon us, nor in that song of

Hezekiah; and I hold that this can be proved by clear arguments: for in the verses, "Wilt thou do wonders to the dead?" etc., and "What advantage is there in my blood?" etc., either Christ the head of believers, or the Church his body speaks, shunning and deprecating *death* as something horrid and detestable. This too is done by Hezekiah in his song. Why do they shudder so at the name of *death* if they feel God to be merciful and gracious to them? Is it because they are no more to be anything? But they will escape from this turbulent world, and instead of inimical temptations and disquietude, will have the greatest ease and blessed rest. And as they will be nothing, they will feel no evil, and will be awakened at the proper time to glory, which is neither delayed by their death, nor hastened by their life. Let us turn to the examples of other saints, and see how they felt on the subject. When Noah dies he does not deplore his wretched lot. Abraham does not lament. Jacob, even during his last breath, rejoices in waiting for the salvation of the Lord. Job sheds no tears. Moses, when informed by the Lord that his last hour is at hand, is not moved. All, as far as we can see, embrace death with a ready mind. The words in which the saints answer the call of the Lord uniformly are, "Here I am, Lord!"

There must, therefore, be something which compels Christ and his followers to such complaints. There is no doubt that Christ, when he offered himself to suffer in our stead, had to contend with the power of the devil, with the torments of hell, and the pains of death. All these things were to be done in our nature, that they might lose the right which they had in us. In this contest, therefore, when He was satisfying the rigor and severity of the Divine justice, when he was engaged with hell, death, and the devil, he entreated the Father not to abandon him in such straits, not to give him over to the power of death, asking nothing more of the Father than that our weakness, which he bore in his own body, might be freed from the power of the devil and of death. The faith on which we now lean is that the penalty of sin committed in our nature, and which was to be paid in the same nature, in order to satisfy the Divine justice, was paid and discharged in the flesh of Christ, which was ours. Christ, therefore, does not deprecate death, but that grievous sense of the severity of God with which, on our account, he was to be seized by death. Would you know from what feeling his utterance proceeded? I cannot express it better than he himself did, in another form, when he exclaimed, "Father, Father, why hast thou forsaken me?"

Those, therefore, who are dead and buried, and carried into the land of forgetfulness, He calls "forsaken of God." In this way the saints, taught by the Spirit of God, will not use these expressions in order to avert death, when coming as the call of God, but to deprecate the judgment, anger, and severity of God, with which they feel themselves to be seized by means of death. That this may not seem an invention of my own, I ask, whether a believer would call simple natural death "the wrath and terror of God?" I do not think they will be so shameless as to affirm this. But in the same passage the Prophet thus interprets that death, "Thy wrath, O God, has passed over me, and the terrors of death have troubled me" (Psa. 88:7). And he adds many other things applicable to the Divine anger. In another passage, the words are, "Since there is force (*momentum*) in his indignation, and life in his favor" (Psa. 30:6). But I exhort my readers to have recourse to the sacred volume, that from the two entire Psalms and the Song they may satisfy themselves. Thus there will be no gloss, and I feel sure of the concurrence of those who read with judgment.

We conclude, therefore, that in these passages *death* is equivalent to a feeling of the anger and judgment of God, and being disturbed and alarmed by this feeling. Thus Hezekiah, when he saw that he was leaving his kingdom exposed to the insult and devastation of the enemy, and leaving no offspring from which the hope of the Gentiles might descend, was filled with anxiety, by these signs of an angry and punishing God, not at the terror of death, which he afterwards overcame without any deprecation. On the whole, I acknowledge that death in itself is an evil, when it is the curse and penalty of sin, and is both itself full of terror and desolation, and drives those to despair who feel that it is inflicted on them by an angry and punishing God. The only thing which can temper the bitterness of its agonies is to know that God is our Father, and that we have Christ for our leader and companion. Those devoid of this alleviation regard death as confusion and eternal perdition, and therefore cannot praise God in their death.

The verse, "*The dead* will not praise thee," etc., concludes the praises of the people, when giving thanks to God for having by His hand protected them from danger. Its meaning is this: Had the Lord permitted us to be oppressed, and to fall into the power of the enemy, they would have insulted His Name, and boasted that they had overcome the God of Israel; but now, when the Lord has repelled and crushed their proud spirit, when he has delivered us from their cruelty by a strong hand and uplifted arm, the Gentiles cannot ask, "Where is their God?" He has shown himself to be truly the living God! Nor can there be any doubt of his mercy, which he has so wondrously exhibited. And here those are called "dead" and "forsaken of God," who have not felt his agency and kindness towards them, as if he had delivered up his people to the lust and ferocity of the ungodly.

This view is plainly confirmed by a speech which occurs in the Book of Baruch, or at least the book which bears his name:

> Open thine eyes and see: for not the dead who are in hell (*infernus*), whose spirit has been torn from their

> bowels, will ascribe glory and justice to God; but the soul which, sad for the magnitude of the evil, walks bent and weak, and the failing eyes and the hungry soul will give glory (2:17).

Here we undoubtedly see that, under the names of "dead" are included those who, afflicted and crushed by God, have gone away into destruction; and that the sad, bent, and weak soul, is that which, failing in its own strength, and having no confidence in itself, runs to the Lord, calls upon him, and from him expects assistance. Any one who will regard all these things as *prosopopoeia*, will find an easy method of explaining them, substituting things for persons, and death for dead, the meaning will be: The Lord does not obtain praise for mercy and goodness when he afflicts, destroys, and punishes (though the punishment is just), but then only creates a people for himself, who sing and celebrate the praise of his goodness, when he delivers and restores the hopes of those who were afflicted, bruised, and at despair. But lest they should cavil, and allege that we are having recourse to allegory, and figurative interpretations, I add, that the words may be taken without a figure.

I said that they act erroneously in concluding, from these passages, that *saints after death* desist from the praises of God, and that "praise" rather means *making mention* of the goodness of God, and *proclaiming* his benefits among others.

The words not only admit, but necessarily require this meaning. For to announce, and narrate, and make known, as a father to his children, is not merely to have a mental conception of the Divine glory, but is to celebrate it with the lips that others may hear. Should they here rejoin that they have it in their power to do the same thing, if (as we believe) they are with God in paradise, I answer, that to be in paradise, and live with God, is not to speak to each other, and be heard by each other, but is only to enjoy God, to feel his good will, and rest in him. If some Morpheus has revealed this to them in a dream, let them keep their certainty to themselves! I will not take part in those tortuous questions, which only foster disputation, and minister not to piety. The object of Ecclesiastes is not to show that the souls of the dead perish, but while he exhorts us early, and as we have opportunity, to confess God, he at the same time teaches that there is no time of confessing after death; that is, that there is then no time for *repentance*. If any of them still asks, What is to become of the sons of perdition? That is no matter of ours. I answer for believers, "They shall not die, but live, and show forth the works of the Lord" (Psa. 118:17). And, "Those who dwell in His house will praise him for ever and ever" (Psa. 84:5).

The *sixth* passage which they adduce is, "I will praise the Lord in my life; I will sing unto my God as long as I have being" (Psa. 144:2). On this they argue, If he is to praise the Lord in life, and while he has being, he will not praise him after life, and when he has no being! Since I think they speak thus in mere jest and sport, I will take them up in their own humor. When Virgil's Aeneas promised gratitude to his hostess as long as memory should remain, did he intimate that he was one day to lose his memory? When he said, "While life shall animate these limbs," did he not think that he would feel grateful, even among the Manes, in those fabled plains? Far be it from us to allow them to wrest the passage, so as to fall into the heresy of Helvidius! I will now speak seriously. Lest they pretend that I have not given equal for equal, I will render fivefold:

- "My God, I will confess to thee for ever" (Psa. 30:12).
- "I will bless the Lord at all times; his praise shall always be in my mouth" (Psa. 34:1).
- "I will confess to thee for ever, for thou didst it" (Psa. 52:9).
- "I will praise thy name for ever and ever" (Psa. 145:1).
- "So will I sing praise unto thy name for ever, that I may daily perform my vows" (Psa. 111:8).

They lately claimed David as their friend! Do they now perceive how strenuously he assails them? Have done, then, with arguments which are merely framed out of garbled passages or fragments!

Their *seventh* passage is, "Cease from me and I shall be strengthened, until I go and be no more" (Psa. 34:14).

To this they join the passage of Job,

> Send me away that I may for a little bewail my sorrow, before I go and return not; to the darksome land, a land armed with the blackness of death, a land of misery and darkness, where is the shadow of death, and no order, and where eternal horror dwells (10:20–22).

All this is irrelevant. The words are full of smart and anxiety of conscience, truly expressing, and, as it were, graphically depicting the feeling of those who, smitten with the terror of the Divine judgment, are no longer able to bear the hand of God. And they pray, that if they deserve to be cast off by God, they may at least be permitted to breathe a little from the anger of God, by which they are agitated, and that under extreme despair. Nor is it strange that the holy servants of God are brought to this, for the Lord mortifies and quickens them, takes them down to the lower regions, and brings them back. The expression "not to be," is equivalent to *being estranged from God*. For if he is the only being who truly is, those truly are not who are not in him; because they are perpetually cast down and discarded from his presence.

Then I see not why the mode of expression should be so offensive to them, when they are not said to be *absolutely dead*, but dead only with reference to men. For they are no longer with men, nor in the presence of men, but only with God. Thus (to explain in one word) "not to be" is *not to be visibly existing*, as expressed in the passage of Jeremiah, "A voice was heard in Ramah, Rachel weeping for her children, and would not be comforted, for they are not" (31:15; Matt. 2:18).

* * *

Let us now consider the remaining passages taken from the history of Job. We have touched on some in passing as they occurred. The first is from Job 3:11–19:

> Why did I not die in the womb? Why did I not perish at my birth? Why was I taken upon the knee and placed at the breast? For now, sleeping, I would be silent and rest in my sleep with the kings and rulers of the earth who build deserts for themselves, or with princes, who possess gold and fill their houses with silver, or as an abortive hidden thing would not exist, but be like those who were conceived, but never saw the light. There the wicked have ceased from turmoil, and the weary are at rest; and those once bound, freed from molestation, have not heard the

voice of the oppressor. The small and the great are there, and the slave is free from his master.

What if I should retort with the 14th chapter of Isaiah, where "*the dead*" are described as coming forth from their tombs and going to meet the king of Babylon, and thus addressing him, "Lo! thou art humbled like us," etc. I would have as good ground to argue that the dead feel and understand, as they have to infer that they have lost all power of perception. But I make them welcome to all such trifling. In explaining the passage which they quote, we shall not find much difficulty, if we do not make labyrinths for ourselves.

Job, when pressed with sore affliction, and in a manner borne down by the load, sees only his present misery, and makes it not only the greatest of all afflictions, but almost the only affliction. He shudders not at death, nay, he longs for it as putting all on an equal footing, as ending the tyranny of kings and the oppression of slaves, as, in short, the final goal, at which every one may lay aside the condition which has been allotted him in this life. Thus he hopes that he himself will see the end of his calamity; meanwhile, he considers not on what terms he is to live there, what he is to do, what to suffer. He only longs earnestly for a change of his present state, as is usual with those who are pressed and borne down with any grievous distress. For if, during the scorching summer's heat, we deem winter pleasant, and, on the other hand, when benumbed by the winter's cold, we wish with all our heart; for summer, what will he do who feels the hand of God opposed to him? He will recoil from no evil, provided he can escape the present one. If they are not persuaded of this, there is no wonder. They excerpt and provide themselves with minute passages, but overlook the general scope. Those who have looked distinctly at the whole narrative will, I am confident, approve my explanation.

The *second* passage is Job 7:7–9,

> Remember that my life is wind, and my eye will not return to see good, nor will the eye of man behold me. Thy eyes are upon me, and I shall not subsist. As the cloud is consumed and passes away, so he who has gone down to the lower parts will not reascend.

In these words Job, deploring his calamity before God, exaggerates in this, that no hope of escape is mentioned. He only sees his calamities, which are pursuing him to the grave. Then it occurs to him that a miserable death will be the termination of a calamitous life. For he who feels the hand of God opposed to him cannot think otherwise. From this amplification he excites commiseration, and laments his case before God. I see not what else you can discover in this passage, unless it be that no resurrection is to be expected—a point which this is not the place to discuss.

The *third* passage is Job 17:1: "The grave alone remains for me." Again, "Everything of mine shall descend into the depths of hell" (*infernus*). This, indeed, is most true. For nothing better remains for him who has not God propitious, as Job then thought to be his case, than hell and death. Therefore, when he had run over the whole story of his misery, he says that the last act is confusion. And this is the end of those on whom God lays His hand. For there is death in his anger, and life in his mercy! This is not inelegantly stated by Ecclesiasticus when he says, "The life of a man is in the number of his days, but the days of Israel are innumerable" (37:28). But as the authority of that writer is doubtful, let us leave him, and listen to a prophet, admirably teaching the same thing, in his own words,

> He hath broken my strength in its course, he hath shortened my days: but I said, O Lord, take me not away in the midst of my days. Thy years are eternal. Heaven and earth, which thou didst found of old, shall perish; like a vesture shall they be folded up (Psa. 102:24–26).

Thus far he has shown how fleeting and frail the condition of man is, and how nothing under the heavens is stable, seeing they too are verging on destruction. He afterwards adds, "But thou art, and thy years shall not end.

The sons of thy servants shall dwell, and their posterity shall be established before thee" (Psa. 102:27–28).

We here see how he connects the salvation of the righteous with the eternity of God. As often, therefore, as they bring forward Job, afflicted by the hand of God and almost desperate, representing that nothing is left to him but death and the grave, I will answer, that while God is angry, this is the only end that awaits us, and that his mercy consists in rescuing us from the jaws of death.

The *fourth* passage is Job 34:14: "If He will direct his heart to him, he will draw the spirit and breath of man to himself; at the same time all flesh shall fail, and man shall return to ashes."

If these words are understood of the judgment, as if it were said, that by His anger man is dissolved, cut down, confounded, and brought to nothing, I will grant them more than they ask. If they understand that *the spirit*, that is, *the soul*, at death returns to God, and that *the breath (flatus)*, that is, the power of motion or the vital action, withdraws from man, I have no objection. If they contend that the soul perishes, I oppose them strenuously, although the meaning of the Hebrew is somewhat different. But, contented with disposing of their cavils, I will not pursue the matter farther.

They brandish some other darts, but they are pointless. They give no stroke, and they do not even cause much fear. For they quote some passages which, besides being irrelevant, are taken from books of doubtful authority, as the Fourth of Esdras and the Second of the Maccabees. To these, the answer we gave in discoursing of the resurrection is sufficient. In one thing their procedure is shameless, and is seen by all to be so, namely, in claiming Esdras, though he is wholly on our side. And they are not ashamed to bring forward the books of the Maccabees, where dead Jeremiah prays to the Lord on behalf of his warring people; and where prayers are made for the dead, that they may be delivered from their sins! Possibly they have other arguments, but they are unknown to me, as it has not been my lot to see all their fictions. I have not intentionally omitted anything which might mislead, or make any impression on the simple.

* * *

I again desire all my readers, if I shall have any, to remember that the Catabaptists (whom, as embodying all kinds of abominations, it is sufficient to have named) are the authors of this famous dogma. Well may we suspect anything that proceeds from such a forge—a forge which has already fabricated, and is daily fabricating, so many monsters.

Made in United States
North Haven, CT
13 March 2024